The Making of Me

The Making of Me

A WRITER'S CHILDHOOD

Robert Westall

Compiled and edited by Lindy McKinnel

CATNIP BOOKS
Published by Catnip Publishing Ltd
Islington Business Centre
3–5 Islington High Street
London N1 9LQ

First published 2006
1 3 5 7 9 10 8 6 4 2

A CIP catalogue record for this book is available from the British Library
ISBN 10: 1 84647 008 0
ISBN 13: 978-1-84647-008-0

Printed in Poland

www.catnippublishing.co.uk

For Bob,
In Loving Memory

The Rose is Red, the Leaf is Green
Here is my work for to be seen.
The Leaf is Green, the Rose is Red,
This is my work when I am dead.

So like the damask rose you see,
Or like the blossom on the tree,
Or like the dainty flower in May,
Or like the morning to the day,
Or like the sun, or like the shade,
Or like the ground which Jonas had;
Even such is Man, whose thread is spun,
Drawn out, and cut, and so is done.

The rose withers, the blossom blasteth,
The flower fades, the morning hasteth,
The sun sets, the shadow flies,
The gourd consumes and Man he dies.

From a sampler in Lacock Abbey,
made by Elenor Cleavland
in the 11th year of her age
May 8
1782

Contents

PREFACE   1

PART ONE 1929–1939 THE MAKING OF ME

Chapter One   Dreamtime   5
Chapter Two   My Grandparents   8
Chapter Three   My Parents   18
Chapter Four   The Island   26
Chapter Five   The Oily Wizard   35
Chapter Six   The Wheedler   42
Chapter Seven   A Whole World   47
Chapter Eight   18 Balkwell Green and 57 Chirton West View   52
Chapter Nine   Infant School   57
Chapter Ten   Fifty-fafty   64
Chapter Eleven   Barney Boko   76
Chapter Twelve   Germs   85
Chapter Thirteen   Going Round the Town   91
Chapter Fourteen   A State of War   100

PART TWO 1940–1948 WAR, PEACE AND TYNEMOUTH HIGH SCHOOL

Chapter Fifteen   The Battle for Britain   113
Chapter Sixteen   Grandfather Westall   124
Chapter Seventeen   The Spectre of Specky-Four-Eyes   129

Chapter Eighteen	Enemies and Allies	136
Chapter Nineteen	Religion and Church Life	145
Chapter Twenty	Rugby	158

PART THREE 1948–1957 FURTHER EDUCATION
| Chapter Twenty-One | Early Writing | 169 |

PART FOUR 1958–1993 MARRIAGE, CHRISTOPHER AND
'THE MACHINE GUNNERS'
| Chapter Twenty-Two | 'The Machine-Gunners' and Marni | 181 |

POSTSCRIPT	197
BIBLIOGRAPHY	200
ABOUT LINDY MCKINNEL	201
SEVEN STORIES, THE CENTRE FOR CHILDREN'S BOOKS	206

Preface

Robert Westall never attempted to write his autobiography, apart from a contribution to the Autobiographical Series, 'Something About the Author', for the Gale Research Company in Detroit, Michigan, USA. However, after his death in 1993, his agent and literary executor Laura Cecil and I discovered many autobiographical pieces of writing among his papers.

I have collated these pieces, placing them in chronological order and, using the 'Something About the Author' article as a basis for this book, have inserted the pieces that illustrate the major periods of Bob's young life. I have used previously published stories as well, notably Chapters Seven and Ten, as they are largely autobiographical. I have also used Bob's experience as a boy on Tyneside, during the Second World War, previously published in his book *Children of the Blitz*.

It was a great privilege for me to know Bob well for some twenty-seven years of his life, and to be in the position now to be able to produce this book.

Lindy McKinnel
Lymm, Cheshire

Robert Atkinson Westall was born on 7 October, 1929 at 7 Vicarage Street, North Shields, Northumberland.

PART ONE

1929–1939 The Making of Me

CHAPTER ONE

Dreamtime

The beginning is a dream: a dream of invincible happiness. It persisted right through my childhood until I was a young man. It always came as I was dropping off to sleep, and it was always exactly the same. It differed from my other dreams and nightmares because nobody else ever came into it. It was simply an experience of falling head over heels through endless blackness. It should have brought terror, except that I was falling very slowly, turning over and over as in a slowed-down movie, and the darkness was deliciously warm. And I had no fear of hitting the bottom, because I knew the bottom was a warm soft trampoline that would send me spinning upwards again in an exhilarating way. There were sounds: huge watery sounds like the running of streams and the roaring of the sea. And my happiness was total and invincible.

I have never told anybody before, because I later worked out that the dream was a memory of how it was before birth, and I thought that if I told people they would think I was mad. But now some psychologists hold that having memories of before birth is a quite tenable proposition.

Because I have known total invincible happiness, I am always on the lookout for it again. I often shudder to think that my paradise was only my mother's vulnerable body that might have been ended in a flash by a fall or accident. I look for it again: it makes it easy for me to believe in my Christian heaven. Death, at most, will be a slow retreat back into that endless joyful twisting and turning.

In my second dream memory I am buried inside the foundations of a house, struggling to get out into the light of day. The foundations are of a deep-red brick. There is a tunnel through them, a kind of maze, full of right-angled corners that are narrow and hard to wriggle round. I get very near to panic, but I manage to contain it and keep on wriggling. In the end I get my head and shoulders out and just lie there, gawping at the blinding light and breathing gratefully, with my body and legs still inside the foundations.

I think this is a memory of birth. This theory too is now quite respectable in psychological circles. It left its mark on me as a child, as an adult and as a writer. As a child I could never bear to be hugged tightly. I used to kick and yell and shout, 'Don't struggle me! Don't struggle me!' In my writing, situations of close physical context are always of combat, struggle and horror.

I am an optimist but at heart I am a loner. I make forays out from fortress-me and grab at my heart's desires and drag them back inside to brood over them. I drag my hurts inside and brood over them, too. Ask me how I have fun, and I would say people. Ask me how I recharge myself and I would say alone, with a cat on my knee and Bach's Double Violin Concerto and a single glass of whisky. I don't mind someone else being in the room providing they don't get too noisy. If I were sent to prison, I'd choose solitary, with books.

This means that there is so much about people I can never understand. Sibling rivalry seems like madness. I have no desire to keep up with any possible Joneses. I do not need the approval of a peer group. I shun fellow writers. I'd rather sit in a cafe in a strange town, an ignored stranger, while the old ladies come in with their shopping and get on with their chat, treating me as of no more significance than a hat-stand. Old ladies' talk, anybody's talk, is totally fascinating.

Nutritionists say our bodies are what we eat. I say our minds, even our souls, are what we absorb, perhaps even before birth. Of course, our minds can spit things out again, like our mouths. What we spit out we do not become. What we absorb we can twist and change, as our bodies digest food. We turn facts inside us into lies, myths and legends, but they remain the truth about us. I am the lies I have told myself. I shall try to dig out the truth and if it is not the truth about the world, it is the truth about the making of me.

CHAPTER TWO

My Grandparents

Lies, myths and legends are not the work of one generation only. I am the lies I told myself about my grandfathers' lies too. I was the child of loss and endurance and carefulness; in biblical terms, a son of consolation. A pretty big burden for an only child.

My Leggett forebears, on my mother's side, were Trinity House pilots. One, according to family legend, brought into harbour the shot-and-storm-battered fleet that carried Admiral Lord Nelson's body home for burial in a cask of rum, after the Battle of Trafalgar.

Hard history starts with Grandfather Leggett, prosperous Norfolk master builder. A great Freemason too, and as Master of the Provincial Lodge he wined and dined Edward the Seventh as Prince of Wales. From his photographs he even looked like the king: same high balding forehead and pale-blue eyes, full of imperious Edwardian sadness. Grandfather's eldest sons went to public school and kept the habit of success. George ran a chain of shoe shops and was an alderman, the big wheel of Bishop Auckland and Durham County Council. The mysterious Horace emigrated to America, became a millionaire and owned racehorses. They were people I never met, as remote and magical as King Arthur.

But they got clear before Grandfather's great fall. Around

the turn of the century, Grandfather guaranteed a loan for a friend to the tune of £20,000 which was a lot of money in those days. The false friend failed and fled, and Grandfather lost everything he possessed, overnight. I still shudder at the honourable lunacy of it.

Grandfather was popular. There was a lot of sympathy, and other friends offered him loans to set up in business again. But, unable to face the shame, he fled with his remaining family, two hundred miles up the coast to Tynemouth. He tried to start all over again. But, two hundred miles up the coast, the family were hated as foreign immigrants. Grandfather was hated because he got a job when local men were on the dole. My grandmother dare not hang out her washing as other housewives, because only hers was smeared with filth, only hers was stolen. My grandfather's tools were stolen too, his first day at his job. A week later they were recovered from the river at low tide, covered with mud and ruined with rust. His source of livelihood was gone, but it was the hate behind it from which he never really recovered.

My mother was his last child, born when my grandmother was forty-seven, and she was totally unexpected. She too was a child of consolation, born after his great fall; his favourite. She often spoke of the wonderful intelligence of his conversation on those sunny mornings when she would get up early and have breakfast alone with him before he went to work. Even as a young child, I began to edge away from the burden of her sadness, from her memories of the awful day people came back from his funeral and actually talked and laughed at the funeral tea.

He died just before I was born. From post-operational shock after the removal of a gallstone. Once, when I was

George Leggett (Bob's maternal grandfather)

small, my Aunt Rose took me into her bedroom alone and opened a bedside drawer. There was something inside that rattled hollowly, stonily. She told me to look in the drawer. It was empty, except for a dark-grey marble. Being keen on marbles I picked it up. It was rough, grainy. Then my aunt said:

'That was the gallstone that killed your grandfather.'

I dropped it as if it was red-hot. She was terrified I'd broken the holy relic. With it, I dropped Grandfather Leggett. He became the ghost-grandfather, looking out at me sadly, longingly, from his photograph on the wall. My mother would often say wistfully, 'I wish you'd known him: he would have talked to you.'

I never said it but I was glad he was dead, so that his sad honourable failure couldn't reach out from the photograph

Mrs Leggett (Bob's maternal grandmother) and
Bob's mother clipping the hedge

and infect me. I began to edge away from the whole Leggett side of the family.

Grandmother Leggett didn't help. She was still a great lady in her one long black dress which reached down to her ankles when every other woman's was round her knees. She had a long black coat with a black fur collar, and a black flat hat that she wore even inside our house. She too was a kind of living ghost, carrying bravely and silently the double burden of social downfall and bereavement from years before. Walking endlessly in her long, patient, pointless widowhood from one daughter's house to another. Her one ambition seemed to be to live as long as possible. The only statement I remember her making is that if you walked a lot and ate heartily you would live to a great age. She'd clung to her Norfolk accent, the accent of her greatness, for over forty years of life in Northumberland. She added 'r' in the oddest places and her voice lifted to a peculiar yelp at the end of every sentence. As a child I was always drawing and I dreaded her catching me at it, because no matter how good and clear the drawing of the aeroplane or tank was, she would ask me what I was 'a-drawring'. The one thing I can remember her doing was walking into an elaborate Meccano model I had spent days making, and which was quite plain and visible in the middle of the kitchen floor. She bent it horribly and then accused me of putting it there deliberately to trip her up.

Never can a poor soul have been so loathed by a small boy for so little reason. They tell me now that she never said a cruel word, never raised her voice, never hurt a fly in all her long widowhood. But there was no life in her: she was a ghost-grandmother to match a ghost-grandfather. When she died I couldn't have faked a tear to save my worthless life. I felt a heartless coldness that shocked even me: I was glad she was tidied away. I shrank from all Leggetts as inexplicable, honourable ghostly failures: failure might be infectious. Sources of weakness that I shrank from as from dog-dirt on the pavement.

And yet, did I shrink enough, closing heart and eyes and ears? I write horror stories, ghost stories. I succeed in terrifying people, as my Aunt Rose once terrified me with a marble in an empty drawer. Where do my ghosts, my horrors come from?

There are no ghosts on the Westall side of the family. The Westalls were earthy. Grandfather Westall was a wondrous and fabulous monster, a man of gigantic strength and passion. When his sixth child was born dead (as all the others were, except my father because my grandmother was rhesus negative in the days before anybody understood about such matters) he tore the massive cast-iron cooking stove from its mountings and threw it downstairs in his grief. He had volunteered to fight in the Great War although he was well over age and became shell-shocked at the battle of Caporetto. Towards the end of his life he always wore a black beret with two army badges, rather in the manner of the famous Field Marshal Montgomery. One badge was his own regiment's lamb and flag, the other he had taken from the body of an Austrian soldier he had killed in a bayonet fight. He used to suffer from a repetitive nightmare which consisted of the dead Austrian coming back and demanding his badge. But Granda was a jovial, social man normally. He was often drunk, but held his drink like a gentleman. The signs of drink were a tendency to sing old marching songs, a tendency to give me large and unsuitable presents of money which were instantly confiscated and later returned to him by the rest of the family, and to burst out with self-invented rhymes like:

The boy stood on the burning deck
His feet were full of blisters,
His father stood in Guthrie's bar
With beer flowing down his whiskers.

Granda – in highland dress (Bob's paternal grandfather)

I stood in terror of him, but it was the enthralled delighted terror of the giant in *Jack and the Beanstalk*. His love of military bands which played what he called 'German music', the way that during the war every morning he raised the Union Jack on his flagpole in defiance of the German bombers, saluting it while standing rigidly to attention, ensured that there was

Nana - in highland dress (Bob's paternal grandmother)

never a dull moment with Granda Westall.

His wife, my beloved grandmother, was a fitly Olympian mate. She was built like a tank and would carry me about for miles until I was over three years old. She did everything with a fabulous definiteness. She had started life as a cook in a large house and there was something of Mrs Bridges in

Upstairs Downstairs about Nana. My mother's custard was disappointingly sloppy and runny: my grandmother's was so thick and solid that you could have carved it with a knife and put it in sandwiches. She became the matron of a girls' school. The headmistress was a dragon who sent her teachers about in fear and trembling, and frequently reduced them to tears. When they became so reduced they fled to Nana and she used to give them a cup of tea and hear out their woes. Then she would take up arms on their behalf with the dragon-headmistress. This action would usually end with Nana threatening to resign which somehow always brought the dragon to heel. In the evening Nana would announce, with great satisfaction, 'I handed in my notice again today, but Tempy [the dragon] came off it.'

Nana knew her place but God help anybody who crossed her in that place. And yet she was delightfully feminine. I have her photograph, taken when she was nineteen, and I am more than half in love with it. Even in youth her body was muscular and powerful but her face was beautiful. She had high broad cheekbones, almost Slavic; huge, bold and utterly candid blue eyes without a shadow of doubt or thought of deceit. I would have married her; any man in his senses would have married her; in her depth of strength, endurance, warmth and love she was the ultimate earth mother. She loved her wayward drunken giant with an invincible love. Once, coming home from drinking, he slipped up a back alley to relieve himself (a common habit in those somewhat cruder times). A woman, coming out of her backyard gate, saw him, and instead of, as usual, turning her head away, she reported Granda to the police and had him arrested for indecent exposure. The moment my Nana heard this she went to the woman's house and, after a noisy episode reported by the neighbours, frogmarched the woman by the scruff of the neck down to the police station where the good lady recanted and Granda was released without a stain on his character. All Nana said was, 'Silly bitch – I was at school with her and she was a silly bitch then.'

Granda led her a terrible dance but when he died she came to within an inch of dying from grief. She eventually married again, a widowed Methodist lay preacher who had admired her from a distance since girlhood, and she lived on for another twenty-eight years. I often used to wonder what she made of her pious, piano-playing, teetotal second husband: when he died she grieved, but only in moderation. She was always on my side, and to be near her was perfect safety.

CHAPTER THREE

My Parents

Memory begins, perhaps, before birth. Why else did I have that recurring dream throughout my childhood, of falling backwards through total darkness? Were there noises in the dream? I cannot remember. But there might have been. The noises of wind and water have soothed me all my life. From the walks along Tynemouth pier as a sixth former, when the sound of breaking waves and the hooting of the foghorn cooled my adolescent furies, to the sound of bathwater running away down a distant plughole. And the consolation of noises off. I hate the sterility of total silence. Footsteps, a distant vacuum cleaner, a cough from next door in the night are a blessing. Did I hear such things in the womb? I think perhaps I did. When my wife was pregnant we went to a concert of noisy Mexican music and my son danced to the rhythm in his mother's womb.

One day my mother told me what a terrible time she had giving birth to me. Twenty-eight hours. 'I nearly died having you. You nearly killed me. I risked my life to give you yours.' Oh, God, the impossible mountain of guilt that rose in my heart then. The debt I could never even hope to repay. Did she hope to bind me closer to her, telling me that? It drove me a million miles away, made a gulf she could never again repair. One can only flee such an impossible debt. I fled within, but pretended to stay close to her without. You were

Bob's parents' wedding day 11 September 1926

the first who me made me a liar, Mother. When I kissed you dutifully, I felt like a prostitute all my life. And I felt a mean cheat, and that drove me even further away. And so it goes.

Why couldn't you have told me the truth? That we nearly died together? That I was born weighing ten pounds ten ounces, a fortnight overdue, by forceps delivery, and had a black eye and a damaged arm. Was I reluctant to be born? Did I sense that it would never be as good again? Why couldn't you have told me, triumphantly, 'We nearly didn't make it, but we managed, together'?

But I can forgive you now, Mother. You were only a child of your time, one of the ranks of the Geordie matriarchy. So many of your generation told their sons the same thing. The matriarchal female, getting a grip on her male. The debt

Maggie Alexandra Leggett (Bob's mother)

would only increase. You made me feel guilty that my shoes were dirty, and then you always cleaned them for me. You told me I was hopelessly untidy, and then packed my toys away for me. Geordie men, whether drunks, wife-beaters or merely chronically late for meals, were to be babied from the cradle to the grave. Spoilt, tolerated, indulged nuisances. And all the time you told us it was the women who suffered in this world, who carried the whole world on their long-suffering shoulders. In vain I yelled, at quite a young age, that my father was working sixteen hours a day, that a soldier who had had both his legs blown off in battle suffered as much, if not more, than a woman in childbirth. You just smiled wisely, full of inner knowledge, and shook your head in an utterly final rejection of anything I might think. I was guilty of the original sin of being male.

I sometimes wonder, did women learn the trick of original

sin from the Church, or the Church from women? After all, women have been around much longer than any Church. Both kinds of original sin had the same effect on me: pack my bags like a defaulting debtor and depart for some South America of the mind. Except, of course, that I didn't. I constantly packed my bags and went out slamming the front door. And then hung around outside indecisively. I have spent years in the act of leaving and never yet left. The world outside is bitterly cold without Mother Westall or Mother Church. So one stays, and snipes and quarrels and leaves and comes back. The movement gives the illusion of progress, but is as regular as the swing of a pendulum. An uneasy pendulum. Yet better than the cold outer dark or the suffocating inner warm.

My first clear waking memory comes from when I was too young to walk. I was a great crawler. Crawling seemed to me eminently sensible. You could not fall far, and if you fell it didn't hurt. I was on the beach, sitting in a hole in the warm dry sand, secure as an egg in an egg cup. All around me the giants were playing. Giants in bathing costumes, with bare brown legs through which I could catch glimpses of the distant blue sea and the breaking surf. The giants had quite forgotten me and they were throwing a beach ball from one to the other. I knew that they meant me no harm but I also knew that they had forgotten I was there. They might trample me in their fun at any moment. They might allow the very large ball to bounce on my head. I thought about escape, by crawling through their legs. But that would be more dangerous. So I didn't move, just watched the huge ball passing over me. It crossed the sun, another disc, that hurt my eyes. Dry sand scythed down from the ball, into

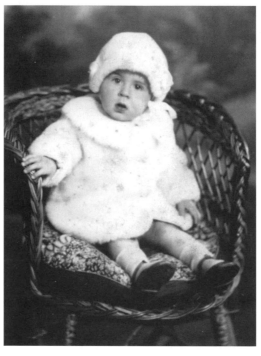

Bob as a baby (1930)

my eyes. Eventually, still ignoring me, they moved down the beach and I was able to crawl the few yards to the safety of the family rug.

The next memory, much more pleasant, is of my pram. I was not fond of walking in my early years. You walked at the bottom of a deep canyon of people, all of whom blocked out the light and few of whom would ever even look at you, let alone listen to you. My pram gave me all the pleasure then that a large and luxurious car gives me today. For one thing it gave me that joy in moving I have always loved, without effort. For another, it raised me from the height of people's knees to well above their waists. The pram and I were always beautifully turned out and I would be admired by a succession of females, the other side of the matriarchal coin. I was, in fact, the Little Prince, and the desire to be a prince has never left me. Secure, the focus of all eyes, I set out to be amusing. This was not difficult at all. One simply listened to what the large people said to each other, and said the same thing, with force and aplomb. At this they shrieked with laughter and opined that I was 'old-fashioned'. This was, and is, a part of my social act that I was never ashamed of. I have always had a quite innocent delight in giving pleasure and making people laugh. The pram had no separate compartment for parcels which were piled at my feet under the coverlet, and by the time we reached home I was usually cramped up double, as my toes played with the sharp shiny edges of the parcels. However, I was convinced that I was guarding the parcels while my mother went into another shop, which made me feel like our dog, who guarded our house.

How does one begin to look at one's father? I begin with a photograph of him, taken when he is seventeen and an apprentice fitter at his beloved North Eastern Marine. He is sitting with two other apprentices, on top of a large piece of machinery which he is helping to take apart. He is wearing a very greasy cap, very greasy overalls, and yet he is unmistakably very good-looking as well as small, about five feet five inches. Almost small enough to be a jockey and certainly good-looking enough to be a girl. As one who has always been very tall and almost ugly, I find it difficult to believe he has anything to do with me at all.

His first employer was a doctor's wife, for whom my grandmother worked as a cook, and he as a bootboy. The doctor's wife used to comment on his beauty and the length of his eyelashes. This did not, however, persuade her to give him more than two shillings a week for an inordinate amount of boot-cleaning.

Such smallness and beauty must not have been assets to an apprentice at the North Eastern Marine, but my father was up to it. He had at that time a temper like a fiend, and a quick pair of fists. He was, as they say, a bit of a lad. He smuggled a bottle of lemonade into the classroom one day and the teacher confiscated it, putting it at the base of the blackboard to torment him for his sins. After two days, the temptation was too great. In her absence, he drank it. Then, to replace the contents, he peed into the bottle and returned it to the blackboard base. There, slowly, as the days passed, it turned first green and then purple. He often wondered what the teacher might be thinking as she looked at it, but she never said.

He once played football for seven hours in loose sand on Tynemouth beach and the following day he could not walk. He once camped a whole summer with friends at Holywell Dene, not only doing his own cooking, but walking ten miles to work every day, and ten miles back. All his life he was a great reader, having a particular love of novels that depicted a man's life from start to finish, a taste that has horrified me ever since. When he was young, if he was caught reading he was clouted, told it was unhealthy and sent out to play like a normal child. The fact that should have dominated his life was that he was born the eldest of six, and all the others died. He said that he spent his childhood following little coffins to the cemetery.

So there you have the two parts of me: the rumbustious Westalls, who lived not wisely but too well, and lived longest.

And on the other side, Grandfather Leggett who seemed alive even though he was dead, and Grandmother Leggett who seemed to me to be dead while she had still many years to live. They are quite enough to account for my spooks, and I suppose I should be grateful. I'm not.

CHAPTER FOUR

The Island

Until I was four, I lived on an island. You might have called it a traffic island, though it held forty terraced houses. It was created by my mother's fear of traffic. I must never go into the road: not even put one foot into the gutter. My parents extracted this promise from me, as they extracted all my very few promises, by enclosing me with their four knees as they sat opposite each other, staring me very hard in the face, and waiting in silence for the promise to come. It gave the moment a solemn holiness, like a coronation. I never broke such promises: they were as promises given to God.

I don't know why my mother was afraid of traffic. In Vicarage Street, where we lived, it was largely composed of delivery boys on bicycles with huge baskets in front. You could always tell the butcher-boys from the grocer-boys because the butcher-boys were pursued by a cluster of sniffing mongrels. Delivery boys in my world were the equivalent of taxi drivers: utterly worldly cynics who wore their caps at a rakish angle, and often smoked while riding. And they whistled: my God, how they whistled. Songs from the shows: 'Let the great big world keep turning' and 'If you were the only girl in the world'. My father said that no musical was a good show unless it had eight tunes that the butcher-boys could whistle. They would sometimes stop and tell me things, for lack of a better audience. What ship had docked; that the mayor was a crook; that their employers were thieving skinflints. This breath of sin I found exciting if incomprehensible: it came from the great world outside my island.

The only other traffic was pulled by horses. The milkman, who was a real farmer from the country, made a daily odyssey into town in his leather gaiters, with his two huge churns of milk. My father said that he left off the lids of the churns when it was raining, to increase the volume of the milk. You took out your milk can to him and he filled it with a ladle, and you gave him the hot tuppence you held in your hand. Once, he offered me a short ride, but he whipped up his horse too fast and I went shooting out of the open back door of his trap, and the milk went flying and tuppence was wasted. Oddly enough, when I got home, my father didn't blame me: he blamed the farmer. He said farmers were all mean and it was his way of selling us more milk.

Then there was the greengrocery-man. A whole laid-out grocery shop on four wheels, with banks of apples, cabbages, tangerines and some scales with brass weights. There was a roof, to keep the produce dry, and pinned round this, on neatly lettered bits of card, were his prices. He was cheaper than the shops, and my mother used him. He went on, even after dark, by the light of four flickering oil lamps, and he would leave you in charge of horse and cart while he went into one of the houses for his tea. It was not his own house: he was a widower, and the house belonged to a widow. He seemed to take for ever over his tea, whereas I could eat mine in about ten minutes. When I asked my father why he took so long, he stopped me going with the greengrocery man, after he had exchanged looks with my mother. I never found out why. But it was a pity I was stopped because if you waited long enough for him to have his tea, he'd let you go back to his stable with him, just round the corner, and you could help him put the horse to bed, by the light of hurricane lamps that flickered above the straw. Horses always tantalized me. My father warned me that they kicked and bit. But if you peered inside their blinkers, they had such gentle, dark, liquid eyes.

Of course, I could leave the safety of Vicarage Street, providing I kept on the pavement. I could turn left on to Howdon Road. But I seldom did. Because the vicarage was there, behind a long high stone wall, black with soot, that stretched like a skyscraper above my head. I think it had broken glass on top, set in concrete. Behind the glass, there showed the tops of high, dark-green sooty trees. Through the crack in the tall green gates, never open, you could see a huge black sooty house: the vicarage. But if you dared to peer through that crack, you stood in mortal danger of the vicar coming up silently behind you, and asking you what you wanted. A tall black pillar of a man, in a skirt that came down to his feet, like a woman's. Cracked black highly polished shoes, and a hint of black sock under the skirt, and a black book in his pale soft wrinkled hands. Hands that my father said had never done a day's work in their life. If I dared lift my eyes, I knew I might see a face without hope of a smile, and a thatch of silver hair. But I never looked: I ran.

It was hard later to realize that this was the man who had married my father and my mother; who had baptized me. His vicarage was more feared by the children than were the high walls of the fever hospital. Nobody I knew ever spoke to him. My parents seldom mentioned him and when they did, they just called him 'Clucas' in the same hostile tone they were later to use for Hitlcr. He seemed to me, at four, an enemy of the people, someone who wished to steal something from all those I knew, though I never found out what that something might have been. Money for church upkeep? Freedom of thought?

Another turn left brought me out on to Coach Lane. Coach Lane was better, worth running the gauntlet of the vicarage for. Coach Lane had steam lorries, that hissed softly when they were parked on their solid rubber tyres. If you put your hand near the front, you could feel the heat coming off the boiler. And Coach Lane had Lionel Clarke's. A bicycle shop, with the added thrill that it lay in a basement and you had to go down twelve steps to it. Rows of bicycles hung vertically on racks, by their front wheels. There was a heavenly odour of oil, which was my father's favourite perfume. Lionel Clarke was a stocky man, in a long brown coat with torn pockets full of oily tools. He usually talked to you without stopping work, often holding a tool in his mouth, but you could always tell what he was saying. He nodded his black hair, stiff as a lavatory brush as he talked, as if he was constantly agreeing with himself. He was as mysteriously my father's friend as the vicar was my father's enemy. He and my father were both men of oil and metal, and they talked of micrometers and thous. If anyone wanted to buy a bike my father said Lionel Clarke would see them right. He was a friend of my cousin Gordon, who was a racing cyclist. All the best racing cyclists wore black leotards then. My cousin couldn't afford one, but my aunt made him one out of an old black bathing costume and a pair of black women's woolly stockings. But Cousin Gordon still won races.

Turn left again and I was in Hylton Street. A short street, largely composed of my Nana's backyard, which was always full of billowing sheets, pegged carefully in position so that their snowy wet bellies missed touching the sooty brickwork by a fraction of an inch. I edge through them: sometimes they reach out and enfold me like clammy ghosts and I am lost in a wilderness of snowy wetness. It's hard to get out for I mustn't mark their whiteness with my dirty fingers. At the point of being smothered to death, I break through and see my Nana chopping up a rabbit for dinner. By her side, on the draining board, is Molly the cat, striped like a dim tiger, fat as a cushion, reaching for bits of rabbit. My Nana discourages her by chopping down on her reaching paw with the meat cleaver, with full force and speed. And always, just in time, Molly pulls back her paw like greased lightning. My father says Molly will one day lose her paw: it will turn up as part of the rabbit pie. But the pair of them have been at the game since long before I was born. They understand each other, those two. Molly has no time for me; she retires to the top of the wall when she sees me. I don't care. At the age of four I don't like cats much: sly cunning things, full of sharp claws and empty of fun.

'Like something?' asks Nana. I am never turned away empty-handed. With Nana, nobody ever is. And she has such exotic cold things in her pantry. The huge mounds of cold custard so stiff that I can carve it into animals, or caves, or a large lump of cold Yorkshire pudding in my hand, to eat like a sandwich on my way home. Or, best of all, cocoa made with two teaspoonfuls of condensed milk. Condensed milk was my first forbidden fruit. My mother does not approve of it: it is sticky, white, fat, yielding and overwhelmingly sweet.

Nana is wonderfully different: strong as an ox, with huge pink arms, suds-ringed, possing the clothes in the poss-tub. It is a marvellous moment when all the washing is done and washing day is over and she upends the poss-tub and her whole yard becomes a raging typhoon of suds, rushing towards the drain, almost overwhelming the tops of my wellies. And when the marvellous Noah's flood is done, and the yard just wet, her huge black bristly yard-broom punishes the cobbles to within an inch of their life.

With Nana everything is fun, even thunderstorms. I remember the day she had me out in the pram and she ran home through the back lanes to avoid a storm. It felt like being in the chariot race in *Ben Hur*.

And so on down the back lane, where the women stand and gossip by their water-closet doors, arms wrapped into the shawls around their shoulders. They are nearly all 'Aunty This' or 'Aunty That'. They pause discreetly in their talk, and keep a benevolent eye on me. If a bigger boy tried to bully me, they would stop him. If he was cheeky, they would clout his ear. And if he told his dad they had clouted him, his dad would clout him again, for being cheeky. The rule of the 'aunties' is absolute but benevolent. If I fell down, they would pick me up. If my knee was bleeding, they would take me into their houses and wash it and bandage it, and give me a drink or a sweet to cheer me up. I like the mystery of their houses, the different smells from the sofas, from the crannies of the kitchens; the mysteries of the fading sad-faced photographs of soldiers in uniform on their mantelpieces. Often I stay for hours. They, with their children grown up, like to have a bairn around the house again. One of them, a pale-faced pretty girl, who is pitied because she has no children, often cooks me chips.

Now into our backyard, where Mrs Cook sits on a wooden crackit, nursing her small, beautiful and feathery dog. As ever, she wears a faded grey beret that balloons out with the bulk of her hair, and a clean pinafore, so often washed that the flowers on it have faded to ghosts. She could be any age, with her wistful faded dreamy blue eyes. Mrs Cook is our next-door neighbour and another widow. She cleans, she cooks, she shares our backyard, she does her washing, and she is visited by women friends who look exactly like her. They talk softly and slowly, with many comfortable silences. They have time just to be. This yard and Mrs Cook were my first outdoor memories. Mrs Cook has always been there. Like God, her existence does not need justifying in my first earthly paradise.

Far off, the hooters go in all the factories. I know every one. I know the gasworks hooter, which means that my father will be home in five minutes.

I run to the corner to meet him. Up the enormous length of Howdon Road I can just see the massive wall of the gasworks, where he is foreman, with the colossal red-brick twin chimneys towering overhead. I have been there once, with my mother, when my dad forgot his bait. It is a magic kingdom where the blacksmith's hammer rings out, where pools of beautiful slick oil, yellow, green and blue, lie on the cobbles, where carthorses stamp in gloom, where men stripped to the waist shovel coal into banks of glowing furnaces. It is my father's magic kingdom, from which he is returning with boots of a fearsome chemical blackness, and a strong whiff of benzene on his cap.

Here he is now, a hundred yards away: I can tell him by his busy foreman's stride, by his quick glances all around him, by his air of carrying the world on his back, like Atlas, and never letting the weight slow him down. Fifty yards off a little boy runs up to him, arms outstretched. I don't know who the little boy is; I doubt my father does. He is just a little boy, wanting a hug. My father grins, stoops down and picks him up, giving him a kiss on the cheek that leaves a sooty mark. Then he puts the boy down, feels in his pocket and gives him a halfpenny. The little boy, without a backward glance, runs for the corner shop.

My father looks up and sees me, and knows that I am jealous. He looks left and right, to check for speeding errand boys, and magically beckons, giving me permission to cross the dread road. Running to him I remember it is Friday night, pay night, when I get my own three pence pocket money. Together, we go into the corner shop. Joe's. Oh, there is a name above the shop front, in golden letters that have cracked and weathered to a glitter more subtle than Tutankhamen's tomb. The name is Nessworthy. But everyone just calls it Joe's.

There is no window display. If you look through the window, past the stuck-on white letters that spell out Fry's Chocolate and Typhoo Tea, you simply see Joe himself. Tall and thin in his long brown coat with his pointed balding head and narrow features. Standing behind a counter of sun-blistered brown vertical planks, with a huge drum of butter that oozes dew where it has been cut, and one of yellow cheese, cut ready into wedges of all sizes. There are scales with gleaming brass weights, and the bacon-slicer where I have so often waited expecting Joe to give us a bloody fingertip among our fresh-cut rashers. But, like Molly's paw, it never happens.

There is a smell of sawdust and of sacking. Sawdust on the floor, with the planks showing through the footprints left by other shoppers. Sacks on the floor, round all the walls, sagging open to show their contents: rice, lentils, flour, washing soda. Tin scoops, some shiny and new, some dull with age, are thrust into the contents of each sack, like a knife into the chest of a murder victim. A ginger cat sits comfortably in the middle of one, washing sawdust off his paws.

Behind Joe's head, the wall is thick with enamel advertisements: Brasso, Oxydol and Robin Starch. There is a 'Mrs Joe' standing always beside him but in my memory she is only a dim ghost. Women move aside to make way for my father. Men are supposed to be always in a hurry. Only women have time to chat; there is always a little collection of them in Joe's, talking of birth and death, marriage and unemployment.

Joe looks at me. 'Now, my little man,' he says.

CHAPTER FIVE

The Oily Wizard

I suppose that all small boys look at their fathers in order to learn what makes a man a man. There must be as many answers as there are men. Certainly I'm glad my father didn't display his manhood by driving large cars too fast, drinking large whiskies too fast, fertilizing a lot of strange women or killing a large number of birds or animals with a smoking shotgun. His magic was infinitely more potent than any of those. In reality, he was the foreman fitter at the local gasworks but to me, aged four or five, he was the oily wizard. It wasn't that he didn't wash as much as anybody else, but mere washing wasn't enough to remove the marks of his oily trade. When he first came home he was often as black as a coal miner; his work clothes, his black greasy cap and dungarees, and especially his dreadful black sooty boots that lived beside the gas stove in the kitchen, smelt of the pit: sulphur and benzene and carbon. Even washed and dressed in his best, he had the swarthy good looks of Rudolph Valentino, the twenties film star. His smell went everywhere before him and lingered after him. On the perilous journey to the outside loo in the dark of a winter's night, with only the comfort of a wavering torch, I would be reassured on arrival to find that lingering smell of benzene. It added to his fascination that he smoked twenty full-strength Capstan cigarettes a day: when he cut me a slice of bread and handed it to me, there would be that comforting faint smell of nicotine on it.

Certainly I never had a trace of the 'wolves under the stairs' syndrome that many children suffer from. The benzene smell banished them. If they dared show their glittering fangs my father would certainly fix them, as he fixed any stubborn engine that refused to work. He wouldn't slaughter them, he would just fix them so they went to the place that was proper for them, and do the things that were proper for them: they'd probably end up behind bars in a benzene-smelling zoo.

The Oily Wizard (Bob's father, Robert Westall Snr)

It added to his fascination that the thumbnail of his right hand grew in five dreadful segments, from where he had hit it with a hammer while he was an apprentice. I would press hard on it to see if I could make it hurt, but he just grinned. He worked in a place eminently suitable for a wizard. It was only a quarter of a mile from home (I got the smell of benzene even when he was at work, if the wind was in the right direction) and sometimes when he forgot his bait I would be sent along with it by my mother. Even this 'bait' was extraordinary, and wizard-like. Something mysterious in a tin, wrapped always in a red-and-white spotted handkerchief. And a tall lidded can, full of an awful mixture of sugar, condensed milk and black tea leaves, which he referred to as his 'makings'.

The works, as I approached, resembled nothing I have come across since except the Black Land of Mordor in Tolkien's *The Lord of the Rings*. A cloud of brown darkness hung over it, always. My father said that was the reason he never had a cold: the germs withered in that blasted air. He said that no child in the primary school that cowered under the walls ever had a cold either, for the same reason. The wall around the works was livid red brick, fifteen feet high, with black iron spikes and broken glass on top. Above the wall thrust two immense red-brick chimneys, day and night belching wreaths of black smoke that sometimes enveloped you as you approached, leaving you coughing helplessly.

There was only one gate, and here lived my only enemy, the timekeeper, a man I deeply hated and distrusted. For one thing he had a clean white face, and a clean white collar with tie. The only work he ever seemed to do was to write things in a large book. Nothing passed the gate but he wrote it down in his book. But, far worse, he had once denied knowing who my father was, the first time I had been sent alone with the bait. What was more, he had made me give him the bait and said he would make enquiries, in a voice that hinted there would be serious trouble all round. Stripped of my sacred trust, for my mother had said that I was to give the bait to no one but my father, I went home in hysterical floods of tears.

Next time I was wiser. Holding my breath, I would duck down and creep beneath the monster's window. This was not easy for in front of that window was a monstrous metal plate, studded with screws and strange writing. The weighbridge, where the coke carts parked as they passed in and out, and my enemy would read a dial inside his office and give out yet another sheet of his endless white paper. If I trod on the weigh-plate, my enemy's dial needle would swing and he would know I was there. So, doubled-up, I would work my way along the six-inch strip of cobble between gatehouse and weigh-plate. I knew he was my father's enemy because my father called everybody else in the works by their Christian name, but this man he simply referred to as 'the timekeeper'.

But now I was safe inside my father's kingdom. Cobbles beneath my feet and, between the cobbles, huge puddles upon which the greeny-yellowy-blue swirls of oil endlessly writhed like jagged snakes. Black brick walls, crusted with soot an inch thick; glass windows smeared with a yellow oily coating so thick you could hardly see an electric light shining through. There were great black doorways from which came the heavy clink of hammers in the darkness; others in which huge, sweating engines turned endlessly, hissing softly to themselves, with no one to tend them. Some huge doorways were full of the dreadful glow of red and yellow light, in which men with shovels toiled, reduced to black skeletons by the glare, feeding the furnaces. Above my head pipes stuck out, puffing huge fat clouds of green smoke, or dripped unknown blackness that might burn your hand away as it touched you. Great stinking heaps of still-hot white ash; pits full of brown bubbling water of a bottomless depth; a weathered, scarcely decipherable sign 'Number Four Retort House'. Sometimes I would wander fearless for ages, until I found a man who had time to speak to me. Fearless, for my father was lord of all this.

I have great respect for Tolkien's *The Lord of the Rings*, and yet I cannot find the fear in it that others feel. Tolkien's Hell was my Heaven. And eventually, a bent dark figure would emerge, white-eyed and white-toothed. No orc, but an honest man, because black-faced. Men with black faces were workers, and my father's friends. Men with clean faces were bosses, or worse still 'Boss's men' and my father's sworn enemies. This blackened figure would recognize me with a cry. 'It's Bobby's bairn!' Others would emerge and take up the chorus. 'Bobby's lad . . . Bob's bairn. He's brought Bobby's bait!' And they would make me feel like the hero that carried the good news from Ghent to Aix. Then the burning question: 'Where's Bobby? Where's Bobby?' was passed from shed to shed, gantry to gantry, until it seemed the only question of importance in the world. Bobby was in number three retort house. Bobby was up on the dread-named coke-crusher. Bobby was on number one conveyor. Bobby seemed to be everywhere, omni-present, like God.

And then he would arrive, hurrying always but flustered never, ramming his way through the day's crises like a little tramp steamer butting through heavy seas, always with a man or two clustering round him as he walked, asking what was to be done, in a stream of wizardly incantation involving cranks and sumps, steam valves and condensers.

Mission accomplished, I would run out of the gate wildly, at full speed across the weighbridge, leaving my enemy the timekeeper mouthing and waving his arms helplessly behind his glass window.

The best time of all was a Saturday morning, when he came off a week of night shift to two days' holiday, while it was still dark at six o'clock in winter. He would be in a mood to celebrate. He would stop at the newsagents and buy me a model cannon he knew I had long coveted. Or else he would call at the baker's and buy bread buns fresh from the oven and bring them to me in bed, still scalding hot and dripping butter (and tasting faintly of benzene). Then he would sit for a few minutes and tell me strange things, like how there were always rats gathered under the railway bridge, and how they would turn and stare at him as he passed, quite bold, their eyes red points in the light of his cycle lamp. The gasworks was full of rats. They used to nibble the hooves of the carthorses as they slept, and the horses, that pulled the coke carts, never seemed to notice. He told me about Ginger, the works cat, who could pick out the one pool of clean rainwater from the many pools of poison, and never came to harm, but the stupid rats couldn't, and burnt their paws and mouth off. Oh, he was an oily wizard indeed, stranger than Gandalf the Grey, and only once broke my heart. I was with my mother in his great engine room, watching him start a great forty-foot engine, by pushing the eight-foot flywheel around with his shoulder. There was a much smaller engine, which seemed an exact replica, four feet long, screwed to the floor nearby, standing silent. I asked what it was for. Divining my lust, he asked me if I wanted it. I said, 'Yes.' He said he would bring it for me when he came off his shift.

I spent eight hours in a fever of expectation, not realizing he was joking. When he arrived without it, I burst into tears and was inconsolable for days. But he did bring me a full-sized model of a Browning machine gun on its own tripod, made in his spare time, for a surprise. And a three-foot scale model of a battle cruiser. Our house was full of the brass working models of machinery that he had made. I had watched him start making a cabinet with wood and when he had finished, a voice came out of the loudspeaker, voices from London and Luxembourg and Hilversum. It was hard for a five-year-old to see just exactly where the magic ended.

He taught me that real men put the world straight when it got broken. Real men created endlessly, out of almost nothing but a few bits of wood and brass pipe and a lick of paint. And he also drew things for me on demand. He could draw a car, or Charlie Chaplin with his bowler hat and cane, or a full-rigged sailing ship. He had a gift for drawing, but thought it only fit to amuse the bairn with. Nevertheless, by the time I got to school, it seemed quite natural to draw. I was quite surprised that everyone couldn't do it.

CHAPTER SIX

The Wheedler

In the power battle that takes place between the ages of one and five, the child has the choice of four weapons: to throw tantrums, to sulk, to wheedle and, most sinister, to Be Ill. I thank God it never occurred to me to Be Ill; all medicines in those days tasted vile beyond belief, and to be inactive in bed, even when really ill, was a torment of tangled sheets.

I tried one or two tantrums. But my father's temper, though seldom roused, was a hurricane. He hit me only three times in my childhood, but his hand was heavy, and the very infrequency of the occasions added to their dreadfulness. I decided in the tantrum stakes I was totally outgunned, and rapidly gave them up.

My parents let me sulk or, rather, they made no reaction to my sulks whatever, and I found that all I was doing was digging myself into a deeper and deeper pit of misery from which I would have a terrible job lifting myself out again.

So I became a wheedler. Not, of course, a stupid wheedler that hits the same button over and over again, and hopes to win by sheer irritation. It did not pay to irritate my father. No, I became an interesting wheedler, constantly changing my position in order to undermine the adult viewpoint. I learnt to use words cleverly, to get my own way. Perhaps my most devastating victory was against my grandfather at about the age of four. I had been left in his charge, while my parents and grandmother went shopping, for the first time. I don't suppose I was very wicked: I probably just went on chattering about everything in my inimitable way, which charmed most people.

Unfortunately, Granda was a time bomb. He had spent four years in the trenches in the First World War and had seen many things he never, ever spoke about, but he groaned in his sleep like a soul in torment. He found the need to soak his shattered nerves in alcohol several times a week. And he was shell-shocked: the tapping lid of a boiling kettle, which sounded like a distant machine gun, was enough to send him off on one of his 'do's'. I presume my bright chattering got on his nerves, because he clouted me. I suppose I reacted with the shocked disbelief of the seldom-clouted, but I must have added a strong dash of my thespian talent, for I am told I turned to him with tears in my eyes and said solemnly and with great dignity, 'Why did you hit me, Grandfather?' looking him straight in the face. It sounds like something from the mouth of Little Willie in *East Lynne* or Little Lord Fauntleroy, in the epic of that name. What it does not sound like is real life, even if uttered in real life: the bad novelist was stirring, even at the age of four.

It floored him totally. The family returned to find him vowing fervently never, never, never to hit the innocent child again; rather as if he had Seen the Light and was Taking the Pledge.

In later days, the Innocent Child made the most of that vow. The family returned on another occasion to find that I had coaxed him into tying my grandmother's clothes line all round the kitchen, and hanging on it every metal utensil available. I stood with an old golf club in each hand, creating a vast cacophony, while he hunched in his armchair, hands over shell-shocked ears.

As the shoot is bent, so the tree grows. The successful tactics of childhood get carried forward into adult life: tycoons throw tantrums in the office; Greta Garbo sulked for forty years; wives all too sinisterly Get Ill. I still wheedle. I wonder if all writers started as wheedlers. Reshapers of the world with an endless flow of words, wearing smooth the sharp rocks of reality?

There is pleasure in wheedling for its own sake, quite apart from material gain. In arguments, I am constantly tempted to take the weakest side and try by words to turn it into the stronger. I could shape you a case for the IRA that would make you weep. I could shape you a case against the IRA that would make you black with rage. Neither would be trustworthy: as a listener you would need to bear in mind 'caveat emptor'. But both the cases would be made of little bits of truth, carefully shaped and dovetailed together to make a great big lie. Only a foolish wheedler starts with lies: once caught out, your case is ruined. You leave your lying for the way you put the truths together; there are enough little truths to be found around the world to make a case for anything, and there is such pleasure in craftsmanship in weaving a really monstrous lie.

I lied a lot in my youth: yet I had my own morality. I seldom lied to get out of trouble, or for material gain. I seldom lied to hurt anybody or to make myself impressive. I lied mainly to make the world a more interesting place for other people: I embroidered anecdotes from long ago and far away that I thought could do no harm. Above all, I investigated how much people would swallow. I plied them with a deadly mixture of incredible but provable truths, and totally convincing lies, daring them openly to catch me out.

All novelists are liars. Successful novelists tell people lies they want to hear. Of all world markets, the market for lies is the biggest and most lucrative. I did not realize what a liar I was, as a novelist, until I came to write a non-fiction book. The endless temptation to clean up somebody else's memories, to make their words flow more smoothly, to leave out a bit of what they said, that lies between two other bits which, if juxtaposed, will make a marvellous ironical ending. You catch yourself, and stop yourself, and the reward of your virtue is that your book becomes less interesting. I shall not try non-fiction again.

You can do much with wheedling: you can make men laugh, you can make men weep; you can make men change the world. But, thank God, there is a point at which wheedling fails: you cannot wheedle a rock or crag, you have to climb it or run away; you cannot wheedle a plank of wood, you've got to cut it; you cannot wheedle a model yacht you have made into sailing straight, you must get the sails right. You cannot wheedle a lunatic into sanity; you cannot wheedle a cat into coming on to your knee (but dogs are suckers for wheedling).

I am grateful for all these things: without their stubbornness, I should long since have become a monster trapped in my own cunning. I remember the way Howard Hughes descended from the genius that faced reality and built and flew the Spruce Goose into his pitiful final days. For wheedling plus money can make anything happen, and God help us when nobody and nothing can say no to us. Rocks and planks, cats and lunatics save me from damnation in a self-dug pit I would not be able to get out of.

Of course, being such a good liar makes me more aware of other practitioners of my trade: I am aware all the time that I wade through swathes of other men's lies. Now, when for the first time in my life I want the truth, I find it very hard to find, even to recognize it when I see it. Truth is usually painful, but then lies can be painful too. I suppose the best test I have found is that truth is indifferent to you; it does not excite you, doesn't try to turn you on. It offers you nothing except itself, like a stone lying in your hand. The truth doesn't demand that you believe it, or do anything about it; it doesn't need you. My niece Anna, when aged eight, said to me, 'You look younger with your spectacles on; they hide the bags under your eyes.' I believed her in a way I have never believed Margaret Thatcher or Ronald Reagan or Billy Graham. She didn't want anything out of me: she had discovered a fact about the world. I shall certainly keep my spectacles on in future. Nor did she wish to hurt me; she wished only to examine me, to find out the truths of me, like when she examines my fingers closely, one by one, and lets them fall through her own tiny fingers.

CHAPTER SEVEN

A Whole World

I didn't want to get up that morning. I curled in a tight warm ball and squinted out at a contemptible world. Everything was destroyed and hateful. There were no curtains up at the window, just the bare curtain rail and great swirls of whitewash on the glass. The floor was bare, cold lino: the carpet was rolled up tightly and tied with string, at the bottom of a pile of other rolled-up carpets. The bedroom sideboard was cluttered with my mother's pots and pans.

My mother came and tried to hug me, but I shook her off. I didn't want to be hugged. Hugging would not help. She dressed me and I did not cooperate, would not hold out my arms and legs properly. She gave me my breakfast porridge. There was no tablecloth on the table, just newspapers. The milk was in the bottle and there was hardly any left. The sugar was in a big crumpled packet. It was as if we'd become slum people overnight. There was no fire in the kitchen range, just grey ash. I couldn't eat. My belly felt jam-full of strangeness.

Suddenly, I began to cry. It surprised me because I never cried, except when I fell down and cut my knee. My face tickled with a warm wet curtain of tears. I cried because I was never going to see Mrs Cook and her dog any more.

My mother took me on her knee; my father, never usually here on a workday, knelt beside me. Their voices were kind, but cross underneath. 'It's a marvellous place we're going to,' said my father. 'It's all green fields. And cows. You can walk to the farm to buy your milk.' This drove me into wilder lamentations. I was terrified of cows. They were as big as houses and they had great sharp horns and they looked at you. And the green fields were littered with dangerous brown circles that looked dry and safe on top, but when you trod on them, wet horrible green stuff oozed out all over your shoes.

'It's all so clean,' said my mother. 'You could eat your breakfast off the pavements.' My grief reached new heights. I had no wish to eat my breakfast off the pavement.

'You'll have your own bedroom,' said my father. 'All to yourself to play in.'

Fresh visions of loneliness flooded into my mind. How awful to wake in the night, and not hear my mother's soft breathing and my father's reassuring snore. And how awful to play alone in a room, when I'd always played with Mrs Cook and her dog.

'There's a bathroom,' said my mother. 'A room with just a bath in. Hot water comes out of the tap whenever you want it. Day or night.'

What horrible lonely magic was this? What could replace bath night in front of the roaring fire in the kitchen range, on the hooky rug, with the radio playing music and the smell of supper cooking and, usually, Mrs Cook's dog jumping round me, poking my wet bare skin with its cold nose?

My father began to lose his temper. He hardly ever hit me, but the quick rage in his voice was worse than any blow.

'What's got into you?' he shouted. But it wasn't a matter of what had got into me, it was a matter of everything that was draining away from me. Like the wave of soapsuds from my mother's poss-tub that ran across my wellies as I waited impatiently for it every washday, turning the backyard into an exciting sea. And then vanished so quickly, so sadly, down the drain. Leaving only the dull yard again.

'The dog,' I burst out. 'Mrs Cook's dog. We're leaving it.' And then my throat suddenly felt like there was a concrete mixer inside it, and I couldn't say any more.

'Lord love the bairn,' said my mother sympathetically. 'He loves that dog.' I think she was close to tears herself.

'Damn the bloody dog,' roared my father, beside himself. 'We've lived cooped up here in two rooms, and now we're going to have five, and green grass and fresh air and fields to play in, and all he can think of is that bloody dog.' He got up and went and stood at the window, staring down the yard, trying to get hold of himself. Then he spun round and said, 'All right, I'll buy you a bloody dog. As soon as we get settled. I was thinking of buying one anyway. Does that please you?'

He stood over me: I think I knew better than to make any more fuss. I shut up, and my mother dried my tears with her pinafore. There was a clop and a rumble from the front street outside. My father looked out and said, 'My father's here, with the horse and cart.'

'Come on', said my mother softly. 'It's time we weren't here. Come and say goodbye to Mrs Cook and her dog.'

Holding her hand, I went.

Mrs Cook was just standing at the bottom of the outside steps that led up to her upstairs flat. She looked . . . helpless. Dear Mrs Cook. Mrs Cook, the childless widow who might have been any age from forty to seventy, in her washed-out pinafore and her beret pulled down to her ears, and her faded blue eyes full of tears. Mrs Cook was always there, in the yard. Like God was in the universe. Only I believed in her a lot more than in God. She was always kind. She cooked me chips specially when my mother was out.

But it was the dog. A middle-sized thin white dog, with long feathery hair and floppy ears, and a tail that always curled round over his back. The dog looked at me hopefully and sadly. I knew the dog knew it was never going to see me again. I rubbed its ears, fighting back the tears. Mrs Cook said, 'You can come back and see him any time, chick! You're always welcome here.'

But I knew we never would come back. I'd never see the yard again that had been the whole world to me. I knew every brick, the huge rusting mangle with the tarpaulin tied over it to keep the rain off, so that you could camp underneath. The twin tin baths that hung on the wall. The outside toilet with the hole in the door, so you could peep out and see who was coming. All . . . gone. The back lanes with washing blowing, where you knew everybody and felt so safe, and Joe's, the corner shop, where you could get four toffees for a halfpenny.

'Say goodbye to Mrs Cook,' said my mother.

'Goodbye,' I gritted out, not looking at her, just playing with the dog's ears. Which was worse, the grinding gargling in my throat, or the spear through my heart? How could you lose a whole world? Your whole world?

Oh, I got my dog, and a good dog he was. Though I lost him too, in the end. And then another dog, because my father was fond of dogs. And, once I had grown up, so many cats.

But I wonder uneasily whether each was just a poor substitute for the last. Or, rather, that with each one I loved, the love got a bit thinner, as if my stock of love was not endless, but that each animal, as it went, took some of my love with it.

Did I ever love, as I loved that first dog (and I cannot even remember his name)? Did I ever love the fresh fields as I loved those brick back lanes? Did I ever love, and accept the love of a woman, as I did with Mrs Cook? Can it possibly be that the Pearly Gates, if I ever reach them, will be set in a sooty brick wall? And that the person who opens them to me will be Mrs Cook, her beret pulled well down over her ears, and her eyes full of joyous tears? And her dog.

Bob and his dog (Rothbury 1938)

CHAPTER EIGHT

18 Balkwell Green and 57 Chirton West View

There is little mystery in our new house. The big windows fill it with sunlight; outside is the endless freshness of gardens, and the green in front where spotlessly clean dogs and children run and play. What mystery and magic there is, is in books in the single bookcase. My father's engineering books, six pale-green volumes, full of wondrous complicated drawings of engines with little coloured flaps to lift up and peer beneath. I cannot begin to understand them; I do not wish to understand them. I just enjoy the pretty shapes, and worship at the shrine of my father's power. It does not seem odd to me at all that my father never consults them: he obviously knows everything that is in them already.

Next to them, the *Home Doctor*, which lays human bodies out in wondrous diagrams, as my father's books lay the engines. No doubt my father understands bodies equally well, for he never looks at that either. Nor does my mother ever look at it; she says it starts her imagining she has every disease under the sun.

Then there is a *Book of the Home*, full of hints on hanging curtains and making jam. My mother's seat of power, which she obviously knows by heart, since she never opens that one either. Then the family photograph album, with my favourite photograph of me, aged two, lecturing some ducks in the park with open mouth and gesturing arms. After that, a *History of Old Tynemouth*, and a thick magazine of King George the Fifth's Jubilee.

The mysteries that come in from outside are all modern mysteries. My father's new greenhouse, piled in sections against the garden fence, smells deliciously of new pine, and with gluey brown sticky dribbles from the knots in the wood that I rub my hand in, so that I can carry the smell of the new greenhouse, pricking and tingling, to bed with me. My father is instantly in command of the new magic, letting me help him put it up. As he is also in command of the cast-iron central-heating boiler for the greenhouse when it arrives. I am allowed to stoke it while he is at work: he shows me how and when to pull the levers, to get rid of the surplus ash, to make the boiler burn brighter and hotter. I am in seventh heaven. As I am with the new radio set with its single grand chrome pillar, and the slit by the dial I can peer through and see the inner world of the set; the shining golden oriental domes of the valves, the red-hot glowing wires. It might be the bowels of a spaceship, en route to Mars.

The boys' magazine my father buys for me is called *Modern Wonder*. Complex drawings of floating docks and biplane airliners, with all the little passengers sitting smugly aboard, and a neat respectful stewardess serving tea en route to Paris. My father and I read it together: he grunting with satisfaction at understanding how the things work, me lost inside the drawings, using the dock to raise sunken treasure galleons or flying to South America aboard the Imperial Airways flying boat *Ceres*. Do either of us realize then, or care, that we are touching each other, yet worlds apart?

My appetite for mysteries is insatiable. It has to be satisfied elsewhere. At 57 Chirton West View.

It must have been called Chirton West View because when first built it looked over the fields to the Georgian country village of Chirton. By the time I got there, the fields had been covered with red brick, and Georgian Chirton was a soot-blackened slum where the poor people lived. The only view to be had from Chirton West View was of the houses across the road with their windows drowned in lace curtains, and their tiny front gardens where undying stunted blackened privet and London Pride fought a goalless draw with scrabbling cats. The knockers were polished every day and shone, the front steps rendered spotless white with rubbing-stone. If any housewife neglected this chore she would be spoken to by the neighbours. If she ignored the hint, she was already on her way down to sluttish disgrace and ostracism. The three-foot gardens stank of cat pee, and the privet and the London Pride never seemed to grow or need cutting. All the houses in the long terrace looked the same but, running on ahead of my mother, I was able to pick out my aunt's house, even before I could read numbers, by the fact that the knob on her front door was black and wondrously shiny, whereas her neighbour's was a creamy yellow.

We always went to my aunt's front door, whereas she always came to our back door. Going to the front door was posher, and avoided the chance of meeting my aunt's neighbours. We were posher than my aunt, and much posher than her neighbours, because my uncle was a labourer and the neighbour a coal miner and they had no hope of greenhouses and central-heating boilers and new radios, and they lived in a terrace, with backyards. Of course, none of this was ever mentioned: we were just one rung further up the ladder that ended with His Majesty King George the Fifth, God bless him. God's will, if you'd asked me.

My aunt opens the door in her well-packed flowered pinny. My father says my aunt is built like a bullock, that she is getting a belly like a poisoned pup. A strong woman, your Rosie. Yet I would never have thought of her as fat. When she hugged me, she felt as solid as a rock; solid muscle inside corsets that creaked faintly as she bent. She had a strong womanly smell, whereas my mother smelt only of powder and perfume and soap. Of course, they didn't have a bathroom: they took turns in the tin bath in front of the fire on Sunday nights. We had a bathroom.

We go up the dark passage, squeezing past the massed overcoats on the coat hooks. The house smells, but not like ours. It smells old. As if the air itself is old, because doors and windows are never opened. At home ours are open all the time. I'm not quite sure I want to breathe such old air, and hold my breath for as long as I can, then breathe very shallowly as I sit down. The room is long and dark and narrow. The aspidistra and the net curtains get most of the light. The room is full of overlarge furniture; the pictures are not at all like our pictures, which are large and bright, and bought from offers from magazines and framed with passepartout by my father. We have *The Boyhood of Raleigh* and a study of a mare and foal on a windy upland plateau, called *Mother and Son*. My aunt's pictures are small and dim and never looked at, mainly of thatched cottages lurking behind high hedges, towards which small muffled female figures are endlessly making their way: I know they will never get there. And my aunt also has pictures of people who are dead. You can feel their eyes watching you enviously from dark corners.

My aunt offers tea and biscuits, or pop for the bairn. The bairn refuses pop: the bairn will have tea. Even though at home he never has tea, which he dislikes. Tea is more grown-up. I sip it as delicately as my mother sips hers, and listen to my aunt railing against God, the council, or even the government.

CHAPTER NINE

Infant School

My arrival at infant school was one of the most spectacular experiences of my young life. I had no sooner walked in through the elaborate wrought-iron school gates (why do all schools have elaborate gates, forever open, forever useless, except for climbing on?) than I was met from one side by a hail of half-bricks, and from the other by a charging mob of huge young gods with lavatory-brush hair, crudely coloured red and blue jerseys buttoned up to the neck, and huge black boots so shod in iron that they sounded like a charge of carthorses. I cannot convey the *size* of those boys. I was five and they cannot have been more than eight, but they seemed to me then taller than guardsmen, more fearsome than the line-backers of the San Francisco 49'ers. I was convinced that the end of my world had come as I cowered back against the brick gatepost. But the gods had no interest in me: they crashed straight past, into the teeth of the hail of half-bricks being hurled by a similar group of young gods at the far end of the playground. They met in a whirl of combat, slithering to a halt and sending up showers of sparks from their iron feet. Then, in another moment, they were fleeing in disorder, gathering up the half-bricks as they ran, ready to face a charge by the other group of young gods in the opposite direction.

Somewhat reassured by being so completely ignored, as if

I was a fallen leaf or a bird on a tree, I looked round and saw mortals of a more normal size like myself cowering in every nook and cranny made by drainpipes, steps, railings and coke heaps. I hastened to join them. Once again, I learnt that the warring gods were indifferent to me and, as the *I Ching* says, the small get by. So must shrimps cower in the crannies of the rock as sharks swim by: leave the big boys alone and they'll leave you alone.

The big girls, on the other hand, I had long known from my own street. A static society, congregating round gateposts like their mothers, arms folded, fat bottoms on the wall, legs stuck out together, blocking the pavement, endlessly chewing the fat, as Nana would have said. There was both peril and profit in these groups. They considered it their right to boss four- and five-year-old boys about, tell them off for their filthy condition, wipe their noses, threaten to tell their mothers about their misdeeds for the general good of society. And they packed a hefty clout if provoked too far. But they also tended to have in their pockets small, crumpled, greasy paper bags from which they would occasionally lever and offer a sweet in the last stages of sticky decay. They also carried on interminable secret conversations which reduced them to fits of explosive giggles. If you approached them, they suddenly fell silent; if you crept up very quietly, you might hear a few incomprehensible words before they spotted you and shushed each other in a fit of hysterics. There was a great evil and exciting secret here, which kept a fringe of tiny boys around them constantly, advancing and retreating.

The secret certainly had something to do with their skirts. Skirts then were covered by a series of deep frills, each about four inches deep. A sort of series of false skirts. If a small boy lifted the top frill, next to the waistband, he got their attention. If he looked under the next one down, there was a tense giggle, a heightened interest from the whole group. Looking under the third one, you were told you were a filthy evil boy, who would certainly come to no good. And yet they looked at you expectantly, wanting you to go on. The fourth frill produced a scream, the fifth a louder scream. One had a delightful sense of being cheered on to eternal damnation. Then you lifted the last one, the true skirt, and at the same time you ducked, if you were wise, because otherwise you got a stinging slap on the face that would certainly have laid you flat on the pavement. After that, you ran away, but not too far. Because the whole thing would start again, once the girls had got over their shocked outrage. You got the feeling that you were dyed deep with evil, beyond hope, but such evil was definitely what the girls were in the market for. It was to be another five years before I heard about sex, in a dirty

Bob (1935)

song sung by a boy from London, that sink of depravity. I refused to believe a word of it then; the concept was not only unattractive and insanitary, it was physically impossible and I dismissed it as a dismal aberration of a sick mind for another two years.

But now a bell had rung, and we were filing into school. School had reassuring shining parquet floors, and a comforting smell of floor polish. The teacher was a woman in a flowered pinafore who bore a strong general resemblance to my mother. There was a large box of toys in one corner, lying on top of which was a large railway engine, better than any I had come across before. I was put at a table with another new boy, Jackie Robinson, who was thin and weedy, and a lot more nervous than me. Dear Jackie, a born follower; I acquired him instantly. I had begun to reassure him, to show him the ropes before I even knew them myself.

Quite soon, I was called upon to read. I read easily. My father had taught me, quite by accident, when I was four. He would settle me in his lap and read to me from a comic called *Puck*. He was totally relaxed about it because as far as he was concerned, he was simply reading aloud to me. But in a fashion typical of the Board School child that he was, he ran his finger along under the words as he read.

One day, to his amazement, he found I was reading silently, half a page ahead of him. This was treated in the family as a kind of miracle, denoting genius. My parents had obviously boasted of this to my new teacher, and she was testing me out. When I passed the test, the headmistress was immediately summoned and informed, and she expressed gratifying amazement out loud, rather like Simeon in the temple over the infant Jesus.

I was next set a page of sums which, inspired, I did with amazing rapidity. Again, this caused a kind of general exclamation by the whole class about my virtue. Such carryings-on today would probably have got a child lynched in the playground during the next playtime. But my classmates just seemed stunned. I then did another page of sums at great speed: unfortunately this time the teacher decided to mark them. Half of them were found to be wrong, rather taking the gilt off the gingerbread. Somewhat miffed, I slowed down a little, and got the next lot all correct. My position as boy-wonder was now secure.

My achievements seemed to throw the staff off balance. I recall being led around the corridors by the headmistress, who told everyone we met that I was a highly intelligent child. I have to add it did not seem to ruin my character or give me a big head: it simply gave me a pleasant sense of safety, and I relapsed into a quiet smugness that made me very biddable.

Nevertheless, I was a thorn in the flesh of my teacher. I finished everything in half the time the rest of the class took, and at first she didn't know what to do with me. She had to keep on telling me to invent something to do for myself. From this, I think, derives any creativity I may have as a writer and artist. I found a book about the Romans, and could soon draw a mean trireme, and an even more elaborate Roman soldier in full armour. These drawings were put up on the wall by the teacher. People asked me to draw one for them and I churned them out, giving them away quite cheerfully as my father had given his away to me.

As war approached in 1937 I turned to drawing tanks and guns, fighters and bombers. I was greatly intrigued by the new principle of brown and green camouflage. I painted an anti-aircraft gun and lorry passing on a hill. I duly painted it in brown and green camouflage patches. The teacher was thrilled and told me to hurry, as she wanted it on the wall for the inspector's visit. I hurried on, painting the hill behind the gun brown and green also. Much to my chagrin the gun totally vanished, to my, the teacher's and the inspector's total desolation. Still, I'd found out that camouflage worked.

Another experience was infinitely sadder. I soon got tired of drawing the real aeroplanes: I began to invent aeroplanes of my own, filling whole sketchbooks with them. One day a boy called John Graham approached me. Would I swap one of my full sketchbooks for a pile of second-hand comics? I thought he was mad because the sketchbook, once filled, was useless to me and I was about to throw it away. Still, I loved second-hand comics, so I swapped.

A few days later, I was drawing an aeroplane in class, when another boy looked at my drawing and said, 'You're copying one of John Graham's bombers.'

'I am not! I'm inventing it.'

'You're not. John Graham taught you how to draw all your bombers.'

'Prove it!'

'I've seen a book full of his bombers that he drew . . . he's got it at home. He did them at home first and then he taught you.'

Then I knew the use my old sketchbook was being put to. I wasn't outraged, just somehow rather sad for John Graham. How awful that he'd had to give me comics and tell lies to pretend to a gift that flowed out of me like water from a tap. I never split on him: probably our mutual friend still thinks that John Graham taught me to invent bombers.

I've never cheated in my life. All the other sins, yes, but cheating, no. Why should somebody who lives beside a river cut his neighbour's throat for a glass of water? I once watched, in a YMCA hostel, a lad move the balls on the pool table to his advantage while his friend went to fetch a fizzy drink. I remember wondering desperately what satisfaction he got out of cheating. I mean, even if he won the game, he would still know that he'd cheated.

There's nothing so incomprehensible as a sin that you've never been tempted towards.

So by the time I was seven, words and drawings flowed naturally, without sweat. Only one prohibition my father put on me: he convinced me I was no good with wood and metal. I am by nature clumsy with my hands. At woodwork, at grammar school, I fulfilled his worst predictions. I couldn't saw straight. If I tried to plane a block of wood square, it turned into an excellent curved pointed shape suitable for a model yacht, and yet when, in my forties, I took to making three-foot model yachts, I found to my amazement that I could manage. I was no genius, but I got there in the end.

When my father saw my first model sailing catamaran, he was shattered.

'You! Made that! All on your own? I don't believe it.'

Fortunately, by that time I was forty-five, and he was seventy-three and long retired. So he didn't feel threatened by my competition any more.

Even the best parents practise self-defence.

CHAPTER TEN

Fifty-Fafty

Friday afternoons, my mother picked me up from school and we went shopping down the town. Out of our leafy suburb, down into the smoky jungle. Wondrous shops were there, full of dinky toys and pink ladies' corsets. But the poor were there too. Beyond the shops, all down to the river, they got poorer and poorer. In the lower depths they Drank, and had no drains; emptied their soapy washing-up water and worse straight into the furrows of yellow clay paths that trickled, in the end, into the black waters of the Tyne, iridescent with the sick beauty of oil and awash with broken fish boxes caught by boys who had no boots or shoes, and left lying to rot on the cobbled quays. Where dirty women hung out of windows and shouted incomprehensible things as you passed, and did incomprehensible things with sailors, then cut their throats as they slept and lifted their wallets and dropped their bodies straight into the river through trapdoors in their houses.

I don't remember how old I was. I know I had sadly abandoned hope of dragons. I had checked for wolves under the stairs and found only a sack of musty potatoes, and a meter with the faint exciting whiff of gas. But there were still monsters. The lamplighter walking in front of us was a minor wizard. He put up his long pole to the gas lamps and created darkness. It was broad daylight till the gas lamps flared instantly, night gathering around them like smoke.

My own headmaster was a fabulous monster of sorts. Tiny, bent, wizened and silver-haired, we loved him. But the boys said that he had once been a six-foot sergeant major in the Welsh Guards, broad as a house with a voice like a bull. Till the gas got him, in the Battle of the Somme. And down the town there were much more satisfying monsters like Happy Ralph, who lurked at the bottom of Borough Road and rushed out at you with outstretched arms and incoherent cries, whether to embrace you or strangle you nobody ever lingered to find out. On Sundays, Happy Ralph went from church to church, roaming the aisles and terrifying the vicar in his pulpit and the spinsters in their pews.

A trackless safari into the dusk. But not without waterholes. First my Aunt Rose's house, only a little way into the jungle, where people still holystoned their doorsteps and polished their knockers daily. But Aunt Rose was definitely a denizen of the jungle, her living room long and dark as a dungeon, only a pale ghost of daylight trickling in past aspidistra and lace curtain, over the massive overstuffed three-piece suite crowded like cattle in a byre.

She gave us tea, which we balanced on our knees. She stayed on her feet, solid as a bullock in her flowered pinafore, hair in a tight black bun, and railed against God.

At home, God was the God of green grass and fresh air and Sunday best, the vicar in spotless black and white, missions to save the Africans from naked sinfulness and roast beef for dinner after. But down where Aunt Rose lived God prowled like a man-eating tiger, driving good men to drink by killing their young wives with TB, and slaughtering innocent babes in their cradles. And not one of his evil tricks escaped Aunt Rose's eagle eye.

'How could He do it?' she would thunder. 'To a little innocent lamb who had done no wrong?' as she stood against the oaken altar of her sideboard, arrayed with photographs of the dead of whom God had robbed her. I treasured her as I never treasured our vicar. The vicar had God on his side, was teacher's pet. My Aunt Rose stood and thundered, fearless and alone. She couldn't possibly win against God . . . could she? Still, I could imagine her smashing through the Pearly Gates, blazing out accusations like a Medium Tank.

My mother saw it differently. Pale, prim and pious, she sat through Aunt Rose's sermons in silence, and walked silently down the street afterwards. Glancing up slyly I would see a furtive tear trickle down her cheek. Often, afterwards, my father would shout at her, demanding to know why she bothered going to Rose's at all. All she would ever say, white as a stone, was:

'Blood is thicker than water.'

Then I would see the dead sailors' blood, thick as Tate and Lyle syrup, red as Heinz tomato sauce, coiling up through the black oily waters of the Tyne.

Next stop, the Co-op on Howdon Road. Sawdust on the floor, full of footprints where the bare floorboards showed through; sawdust that was carried by departing feet across the wet pavements for miles around. You could have tracked your way to the Co-op without ever raising your head, just by following the sawdust prints. There was a fat black-and-white cat, sitting on a sack of loose dog biscuits, licking sawdust off its fur; whole sides of smelly bacon, hanging from floor to ceiling; round blocks of dewy butter and cheese, big as barrels; gleaming brass weights and Jack Sylph.

Jack Sylph was also a magic monster, more magic even than my aunt. I knew from poems that I'd learnt that a sylph was a slender naked female. Jack, though undeniably thin was also undeniably male, and clad in a long brown coat, with a yellow pencil behind his ear. And though his face was young he was as totally bald as a polished egg. Did he polish his head every morning with a duster, after he'd cleaned his teeth? Did he use furniture polish on it? As my aunt used polish on the photo frames of her Dead? My mother said he'd been bald ever since he was eighteen, yet he had courted and married and had four children. I thought of his wife, waking up in the dark, and feeling for that warm bald polished egg, as I still reached for my teddy bear.

Jack was a wizard too. He could cut you a piece of cheese any weight you wanted. My mother always asked for odd weights, just for the pleasure of seeing him do it.

'Six and three-quarter ounces, please, Jack.' He draws himself up to a great height, his eyes as keen as Don Bradman scoring a six. Down comes the cheese wire. On the scales . . . exactly right. My father says he should be on the music halls.

And he makes up her order without ever stopping asking about her family. 'I'm glad her sciatica's better . . . and a pound of washing soda.' His head talks and all the time his clever white hands are reducing whatever bags, tins, drums or packets she has bought into an exact geometrical cube, wrapped in brown paper and tied with string, with a double loop at the top for her to put her fingers through to carry it.

Next, to Tawse's the drapers, where my mother used to work before she married. Tawse's is a cliff, twelve foot high, of shelving behind the counter. There are ladders nearly as high as firemen's ladders, up which assistants run to lift down enormous overwhelming boxes and rolls of cloth. My mother has a huge dent in her shin where she used to lean into the rung of the ladder when she raised both arms to lift something down. Sometimes, on evenings round the fire, I grow fascinated by it, press on it, ask her if it hurts. She doesn't wince. I ask her if she was scared, up the cliff; she says she got used to it.

My mother, after endless pursing of her mouth and feeling the material between finger and thumb, proving to the young chits who are working there now that she is no fool and has been in the business, makes her purchase and hands over her ten-shilling note for a pair of rayon stockings at one-and-eleven-pence-three-farthings.

Now is the big moment. The assistant screws the bill and the note into a round wooden cylinder a bit like a shell. She loads it into a cage . . . I look at the ceiling. There is a kind of miniature tramway screwed along the ceiling. The assistant pulls a lever and the wooden shell whizzes along the tramway like a rocket with a fearful rattle, just like a tram, and vanishes into a mysterious little wooden house marked 'cashier'. After two minutes, the shell comes rocketing back, with the receipted bill and, magically, the correct change in it.

Why does that person hide inside that black wooden box? Has he no legs, like the man who sings songs for money from a little trolley at the top of Saville Street? Or is he hideously deformed, like the midnight mechanics who empty the earth closets in the cart-rumbling lamplit dark and never show themselves by daylight, because their faces are eaten away by unmentionable mysterious diseases?

Out into the rainy street. My mother takes my arm in hers now. For the unemployed men are squatting in groups at every street corner, passing a smouldering fag end between them, smoking it down to the last quarter-inch by impaling it on a pin they take from the lapels of their coats. You can see the heads of a row of pins, gleaming in each of their lapel tops, for they turn up their collars against the drizzle. They pick up the pins from the ground, like they pick up fag ends.

It is not that my mother is afraid of anything the men might do or say to her. They dwell in a world of their own, their heads much nearer the ground, their cracked boots polished till they shine like diamonds, their white mufflers spotless, their caps as sharp-set as the brave soldiers they once were. Wearing their hopeless pride like a wall. No, we did not fear them; but we feared what had happened to them. As if unemployment was infectious, like diphtheria or scarlet fever that could pass through the air from their very breath. My father is employed, at the gasworks. His work-muffler is filthy; he never has time to clean his boots. He is busy working.

Last stop, the chemist's. It glows through the dark like a jewel, huge globes with pointed stoppers, two feet high, full of mysterious liquid, red, blue, green, enough to poison the whole town. And inside, more huge jars with unreadable names. SOD BIC. AQUAE FORTIS. CANT MEM. Rows of varnished drawers full of wickedness.

But the most terrifying thing about the chemist is the way he speaks. He speaks posh, posher than anyone I've ever heard. My mother wants some Sal Hepaticah. I am always encouraging her to buy Sal Hepaticah. Every time we set out for town I ask her whether she has enough. The medicine chest in the bathroom must be full of it; I don't even know what she uses it for. But I long to hear this chemist echo her, with his utterly eerie voice.

'Sal Hair-pair-teeh-caaah.' It sounds like a spell, like the names of one of the Pharaohs in school, or of those volcanoes in Mexico.

In the street again, I chant it to the night. 'Saaaal Heeeeep-eeeeeh-tiiiii-caaaah. Saaaaal Heeeeep-eeeeeh-tiiic-caaaaah.' My mother tells me to stop; it is rude. So I chant 'Tuuuutaaaankaaaamun' and 'Coootooopaaaxi' instead.

And so to Nana's for tea. Her front door opening at a touch; my mother's timid 'Yoohoo' echoing through the church-like gloom of the cold front hall. Then the kitchen door opening, the red light, the blast of heat from the kitchen range, the sweet overpowering smell of baking bread and Nana, up to her elbows in white flour, wiping her pink perspiring forehead with the back of her hand, and adding more white streaks to what is there already. Behind her, the kitchen range gleams black and silver in the red gloom, and on the mantelpiece all the horse brasses and ornaments, polished till they too gleam silver. Nana polishes things to within an inch of their life.

Half the table oilcloth is covered already with the plump white female shapes of finished bread, cooling on wire grids. Inside the gleaming brass fender, great cloth-covered bowls, where domes of white female dough rise inexorably every time you lift the cloth to peep. And yet more white dough, twisting between Nana's strong hands.

'Sit yourselves down,' she says with a gasp of exhausted glee. 'Give the bairn a bun, while they're hot.'

At home, I might be made to wait. Not here. Here I am a little king. I can have all the buns I can eat. Instantly. Till I am sick, though I never am. That is her way, that is part of her magic.

The smell of the opened bun, the smell of the running, melting butter; the heat of the fire on my face, turning to pricks of perspiration on the back of my neck. The black horsehair sofa prickles against the backs of my knees, under my short trousers. My grandmother is a white breadwitch, solid and strong as her rising dough, and I am safe in her kingdom.

When I was born, my mother had a bad time. She often tells me and I feel dreadful guilt. Afterwards, she was too weak to carry me in her arms. But my grandmother carried me about everywhere, till I was three. My father often says, in a quietly glad voice, 'Your Nana's a strong woman.'

Yet she's as quick to joke as a child. Once, when my grandfather was washing at the kitchen sink, stripped to the waist, after work, she held a handful of snow against his bare back. His mouth flew open with the shock. His false teeth fell out and Nana still gets helpless with laughter when she remembers.

Sometimes, she still takes in stray men as lodgers. Lost dogs, down on their luck. An ex-army major, full of wondrous stories about pig-sticking in India, but often still shell-shocked and shaking with black memories of the trenches. The first Oriental merchant in the town, a carpet-seller called Ali Hassan. He is prospering greatly now, but he still calls every year to bring her a Christmas present. He sits at the table in a turban, with two turbanned grown-up sons standing respectfully behind him, waves his jewelled hands and tells her stories and gives her huge drums of Turkish Delight. The real stuff, not Cadbury's rubbish; wooden boxes with Turkish writing on the side, powdered white, which I share while he is still sitting there. He is more exciting than Charlie Chan on the movies.

My mother realizes she has forgotten to buy my father's cigarettes. 'Run along back, hinny. You've just got time, before he comes,' says Nana.

I am alone with my magic woman.

She says, 'Eeh, where've I put my oven cloth?' I giggle, because I can see it hanging over her shoulder. She follows my eyes, and finds it.

'Eeh, aah'm daft. Aah'd forget me head if it was loose.'

I say, 'Fifty-fafty, you're a dafty.' I wouldn't dare say that to my mother. She would say it was rude. Nana doesn't care. Instead, she says, 'Do you know who Fifty-fafty was?'

'No. It's just something we shout to each other at school. I didn't know it was a person.'

Her eyes grow thoughtful. 'Oh, aye, he was a person all right. Poor bugger. But you don't want to hear about him . . .'

'I do.' I know she is only teasing. There is a story coming up. There is a glint of excitement in her eye.

She draws herself together, like Jack Sylph cutting cheese.

'He was a poor boy. Born down by the river. Fishermen. Hadn't two pennies to bless themselves with.'

I shiver deliciously; they put two pennies on the eyes of dead people.

'Anyway, Fifty-fafty was bright. He could see there wasn't any money in fishin', so he ran away to sea to make his fortune. Just like Bobby Shaftoe. An' when he went, he took his father's silver ring. The family heirloom, the only thing they had worth tuppence.

'Well, they cursed him an' forgot him. All except his sister – he'd been closest to her. An' they got poorer and poorer. Aah can't tell ye the things they had to do to make ends meet.'

I shiver again; I know the things they do, down by the river.

'An' then, one day, years later, this grand rich man comes to the town – wearing a fur coat and so many rings on his fingers it was dazzlin'. He was buyin' drinks for everybody he met. He was the talk of the town. But he had a great beard coverin' his face, an' he wouldn't tell anybody his name. An' that night he wouldn't stay at the inn – he walked down to the river and sought out that family an' asked them if they could put him up for the night. An' they looked at his fur coat an' rings, an' the great bag he carried, an' they said they could. And at supper, and all the time till bedtime, he talks about the places he'd been an' the wonderful things he'd seen, an' of all the ships and land and houses he owned.

'An' just afore bedtime, he catches the sister outside, an' swears her to secrecy an' tells her who he is. It was Fifty-fafty. He showed her the ring an' she believed him, even after all those years. He had come back, like he had promised all those years ago, to make them all rich, so they could live like lords. She begged him to tell everybody straightaway. But he wanted to give them the big surprise he'd worked an' slaved for all those years. An' it was Christmas Eve, an' his big bag was full of presents for them . . . An' she couldn't do nothing about it – cos he'd sworn her to secrecy. So she went to bed, upstairs, with her mam.

'And in the morning, when she came down, her father and brothers were all laughing and winking at each other, and there was no sign of Fifty-fafty. They said he'd had to leave early, to catch a boat on the tide.

'An' then she knew what had happened. They'd killed him in the night, when he was asleep, an' robbed him in the dark. It was his dead body that had sailed out on the tide, not a ship.

'An' then she burst out weeping, and told them about the ring. An' they took out the stuff they'd stolen, an' there was his father's ring they'd slipped off his finger in the dark, and never noticed.

'An' they fell to blaming and quarrelling, and word got to the magistrate an' they were all hanged. When they could've lived like lords.

'An' that's the story of Fifty-fafty.'

She sighed. 'If only he'd listened to his sister.'

I was silent, and she was silent. Then she finished kneading the last of the dough and set it to rise. And I thought of Fifty-fafty, and all his work and all his hopes, and the way he died, his throat cut in the dark, like a beast, on Christmas Eve. And the way, for hundreds of years, he had haunted the schoolyards, with the boys shouting:

'Fifty-fafty, you're a dafty.'

Poor Fifty-fafty, would they never let him rest? Would his daftness live on, to the end of time, in the boot-stamping dead-fly toilets, in the rain-soaked schoolyards?

And then my mother came back with my father's cigarettes. And then my father came from work, all grinning and greasy and black with his job, with his three-pound pay packet in his pocket. And Nana made the fire up and we had a slap-up tea with bacon and egg and new bread. And Nana drew her dark-red velvet curtains against the rain and the dark. And we were snug, as we always were.

But I listened to the wind and the rain, and thought how thin the glass of the window was, and out there was Fifty-fafty, at the bottom of the sea still, his blood that was thicker than water coiling up through the black depths, like the slime from a rotting cod's head. And Jack Sylph who lost all his hair at eighteen, and the unemployed men squatting on the corners when it was not their fault, and the man-eating God who killed good men's young wives with TB and drove them to drink, and my headmaster who had shrunk in the poison gas of the Somme.

And I cried for them all, quite suddenly.

My father was furious with me, saying I was going on like a wet girl. I had never seen him cry; I don't think he ever did. When I told him about Fifty-fafty he said Nana had just told me the story of an old play she'd seen years ago at the old Theatre Royal. That it wasn't true. But why should the boys call out about Fifty-fafty if he was just some old play?

My mother said, rather proudly, that I had too vivid an imagination, just like her. But Nana marvelled at the softness of my heart.

I was glad for once, that night, to get back up into the green suburb. It was some years still, before I realized that God prowled up there as well.

CHAPTER ELEVEN

Barney Boko

The only Latin I remember from my schooldays is *Facilis descensus Avernus*: Easy is the descent into Hell. I fell into Hell educationally when I was eight years old.

When my parents, in 1934, moved to the new Balkwell estate, they were not just looking forward to wide views over the countryside and going to fetch milk straight from the farm. They were also hopeful that they were getting me away from the old junior school in the town centre. And indeed, I spent three happy years at Collingwood Infants, which was modern, airy and strong on open verandas, green playing fields, and pretty young teachers in flowered smocks.

What my parents hadn't realized was that I would move straight from Collingwood Infants to the dreaded Chirton Junior. Chirton stood among the urban slums that my parents had escaped from. It looked like a prison with a tall black perimeter wall, and gothic windows placed so high up you couldn't look out on anything but Oscar Wilde's little patch of blue sky. Collingwood was built by a state that loved children: Chirton by a state that hated children. Collingwood's floors were shining parquet blocks: Chirton's put splinters of wood into your backside every time you had to sit down on them. The interior was dim with green and brown paint with honours boards so old and dark and withered that Robin Hood's name might have appeared on them.

A caning school: a school where they caned all the time. A school we were forced to share with the children of Chirton, who wore steel-tipped boots where we wore shoes, whose hair was cut short and stiff as a lavatory brush to avoid infestation by nits and lice, whose skin was painted purple in patches all over their hands and faces to try to cure the scourge of impetigo. Bluntly, children who, on a wet day, smelt like a dead sheep. If we were put to share a twin desk with a Chirton child, we sat as far away from them as possible, imagining unmentionable things crawling along the polished seat between us. I don't know how much of this prejudice was justified. I don't know how much of it was even our own, as opposed to our parents. Certainly our parents were horrified. They had sacrificed much to leave the Chirtons of this world for ever, and here were their children herded back into it like cattle to the slaughter. The distance from home to Chirton was no more than a quarter of a mile; it felt like the distance to Siberia.

But Hell is not Hell without Satan, and Chirton's Satan was a man called Barnett.

'Bar-nett,' he told us the first morning. 'Remember, a "net" to catch you in.' After that, he caned anybody who called him by the much more common name of Barnard.

Barney Boko was the captain of three hundred tiny souls. Within those walls and spiked gates he had, if not the power of life and death, the power of torment. He dressed beautifully, always in a brown pinstripe suit, shoes polished like patent leather and a spotless white collar and tie. He was a tubby little man and his black hair was smarmed down to a patent-leather skullcap with hair oil. It was his face that gave him away: red as a furnace for ordinary rage, but the world threatened to come to an end when it turned white. His eyes were hot and black and tiny and, behind horn-rimmed spectacles, they roved like homicidal black beetles. It was worst when his spectacles caught the light: you couldn't tell whether he was looking at you or not. His stubby hands were always clenched even when they weren't clenched around the cane. He never shouted, never said a lot; he never waved his arms about or gestured. He had an awful listening stillness, the stillness of a bomb about to go off; the stillness of a steam-boiler when the hand of the pressure gauge is pressed hard against the top of the dial.

He encouraged a stillness in us. If you said nothing, if you did nothing, he couldn't get you. His hot little roving eyes could not pick you out from the class, who huddled like sheep when he appeared. You would feel those hot little eyes roving over you, hot little burning beetles on your skin, which trembled as they passed. Then they would pass on to someone else, and you'd take a deep shuddering breath, daring to breathe again.

To be fair to him, he wasn't after us new estate children who he had parked en masse in the top class of each year. He was after the slum children in the bottom class. I suppose he knew that if he ran amok among the estate children, their parents might complain. The parents of the slum children had other mysterious things to occupy them, like drink and debt, beds left unmade all day and coal kept in the bath: they would no more dream of complaining than of sailing on the *Queen Mary*.

But we weren't spared the public executions. In assembly, having sung 'New every morning is the love', we would sit in stiff rows on the splintery floor, marked with yellow lines for the playing of netball, while some steel-booted lavatory brush was dragged on to the raised platform, and his sins told to us in graphic detail.

'Oswald Hagan killed a cat: strangled it.' And then the cane would descend six, twelve times; the thin hiss through the air and the whack into flesh, while we turned our eyes down to follow the whorls of grain in the splintery yellow-lined floor.

'Oswald Hagan killed an innocent, defenceless, harmless cat,' screamed Mr Barnett, spitting so hard that a speck of his spittle settled on my cheek four rows back, and burnt into my cheek as if it were acid and under those mad bulging black-beetle eyes I didn't dare wipe it away. Then the mayhem started. It seemed to go on for ever, but actually only until Oswald had been beaten into a screaming, foaming-at-the-mouth wreck who refused to stand up and be a man and take any more punishment.

He noticed me early: my name had gone before me. He has been told that I am brilliant. For once he has, in me, the chance of a pupil getting a scholarship to the High School. When, at the end of each term, I am summoned to his room to discuss my report (and many, even in my privileged class, are summoned to be caned) he attempts to be pleasant. He makes his smile, un-real-ly. He makes ponderous jokes and calls me 'Bold Bob' as if he knew something about me that only he and I know. A secret against the world.

I do not want his approval; I do not wish to laugh at his jokes; I do not wish him to wrap me in a private nickname, like a warm wet clinging blanket. But in the buttocks of my soft white bottom, a little cold because the draught from his door is running up the legs of my shorts, I can already feel the cut of his cane. I smile at him, laugh at his jokes, accept the nickname he gives me. For the first time in my life, I am not-me. It is the same as kissing elderly bewhiskered honorary aunts that my mother insists I kiss: but I do not hate the aunts, they only momentarily revolt me.

Him, I hate.

I learnt to be a coward: to hover in the middle of every group and keep my head down. All my creativity was channelled into not being caned by Mr Barnett. But I was not to be left in the middle of my group. Mr Barnett did not get many pupils into the local grammar school on a scholarship. So he regarded me as the prize pig, the goose which was going to lay the golden egg. He would stop me in the corridor, his face creased into an expression that I think was meant to be joviality, and ask me how my work was going. I began to work extremely hard, wishing desperately that I could have had the courage to do badly.

He comes, in the second year, to teach us for once. He has read a book on the new italic writing. He arrives in great enthusiasm, with an armful of special new pens and large sheets of paper and bottles of ink he has bought specially with his own money. He is full of enthusiasm, almost benevolent. He explains. We set to work, desperately trying to do exactly what he wants, only half understanding, and not daring to ask the normal questions. He prowls up and down the aisles, impatient for exact beautiful replicas of what he has seen in the book he has read. We begin to sense that we have failed. His eyes, crawling over us, feel hotter and hotter; we begin to hear his breathing getting heavier and heavier.

The boy next to me is the weakling of the class; pale, thin, baby-faced but of a respectable, almost middle-class family.

The shapes that he is making are even worse than anybody else's.

As the tension rises, he is picked out. As Barney Boko will always pick one out. The rest of us listen without lifting our heads from our paper, listen and shudder and feel very relieved it is not us.

'Not that way, boy! Let me show you.' The words are civilized: the hate in them on the point of boiling over. He pushes the boy out of his seat next to me. He sits down instead, hard against me, so I can hear him panting. 'Do it like this, boy. Like this, and this!'

In his rage, he presses too hard. The pen catches in the paper, and spatters ink in all directions. The pen goes right through the paper. He is stabbing the paper to death, because he is not allowed to stab the boy.

Finally he crumples the paper into a ball, and throws it right across the classroom. The violence in the air is like a thunderstorm. Then he seems to catch himself, to pull himself up sharp. He stands up, his voice cold and dead and mechanical. We hand up the pens and bottles of ink and papers, which he crumples and stuffs into the waste-paper basket. Then he stalks out and we have our beloved safe Miss Atkinson back instead. He never tries to teach us anything again. We have been put in the waste-paper basket, with our papers.

The mistresses who take the junior classes are tremblingly kind when Mr Barnett isn't about. And even he can't be caning everybody in every class at once, but teacher and class listen together, shaking, for his footsteps in the corridor.

In my final year, he loads honours on to me. Chief milk monitor, carrying round bags of pennies and counting them exactly right. Head boy. When there is an air raid, I do not form crocodiles with the rest, but pick up the official electric lamp that lies always on my desk, and hurry ahead to put the lights on at the great switchboard that is situated at the far end of the dark labyrinthine air-raid shelter. I am sent out on long journeys to the education office in school time, with important-looking long brown envelopes. Greatly daring, I take time off to look in the busy morning shops on the way back. Once, on a very hot day, I got overheated, and he takes my coat off, with great concern, and holds my wrists under the cold tap in the cloakrooms, to cool me off. That was the one true thing he ever taught me, the one thing I am indebted to him for: I fear he actually, in his mad way, cares for me. I am terribly important to him, especially after I do win the scholarship. It is creepy: the more I have to pretend to reciprocate, the more he is making me into a creep. And yet I knew that if I once rejected his care I would face a holocaust worse than Oswald Hagan when he killed the cat. And all the time I was convinced Mr Barnett was mad, as he twitched with evil rage and black hate, inside that most respectable pinstripe suit. Of course I was quite unable to tell my parents because I didn't know what was going on myself. But I got to hate myself more and more. I had to amaze him with my brilliance constantly, and he was the one person in the world I did not wish to amaze.

And then I twigged what was going on, after the Second World War started, and I saw a newsreel of Hitler playing with his Alsatian dog, and laughing with it, and the dog loving him. Everybody, however mad, however evil, has got to believe that something or somebody loves them.

Mr Barnett was Adolf Hitler in miniature, and I was the Alsatian dog.

It came to a head one morning in his office, while I was giving my correct account of the milk monies. Oswald Hagan and his elder sister Minnie came in late. They were late every morning; they were caned every morning. They were simply especially late that morning, so I was there to see it.

Oswald was already a weeping wreck, shaking from head to foot in anticipation. Minnie pleaded and pleaded to save him from the beating. Blame her, she said, cane her. It was she who had wakened late, she who had failed Oswald. Their mother never wakened up till noon. (She was said by some to be the local lady of ill repute.)

Finally, Minnie turned and appealed to me. Wasn't it fair that Mr Barnett cane her and spare Oswald? I wanted to join in. I wanted to tell dear Mr Barnett exactly what I thought of him. I think he saw it coming: he was no fool. 'That'll be all, Bold Bob,' he said decisively.

Minnie Hagan looked at me pleadingly, as if I was the last trace of a sane outside world. I wished I was a hero; I wished I could break his cane in half, or at least shout at him to have some decency, that there's no point in caning the Hagans every morning in life.

And so I turned and went. I have never forgiven myself. In all the years after I left, even when I was an undergraduate I would get moods of black rage when I would decide to go back and tell him exactly what I thought of him. But I was still deciding to go when I heard that he'd died. He is with me to this day. Always I am in a plot against those in power; always I am searching for their feet of clay: each one is Mr Barnett. It doesn't matter what a man is the head of, a communist country or an English district council, the Anglican Church or the CIA, Imperial Chemical Industries or the British Army. For a man to wish for, let alone to wield power, makes him evil at the root, to be dragged down from his seat if at all possible. Any man in authority is Mr Barnett.

It has made a nonsense of my political life. I have voted for every possible party except the Communists; since I reached voting age I have never voted for the same party in two successive elections. Always I am seeking the lesser of two evils.

It has left a mark on my writing too. My heroes are all fairly brilliant rebels and subversives. Only my heroines, oddly enough, make desperate efforts to hold my bookish worlds together; but then, when I was a child, all my female authority figures were rather nice, and usually pretty into the bargain. I finally killed off Mr Barnett nastily, when I was fifty-five years old, in a ghost story called *The Boys' Toilets*.

CHAPTER TWELVE

Germs

My first encounters with illness were very muddling. For one thing, I confused 'germs' with 'Germans'. Everyone seemed to think they were both a very bad thing. And then again, I had a vision of germs as being rather the size and shape of earwigs, but jet black and with even sharper pincers at the front end. Yet I also knew that they only made you ill if you breathed them in through your nose or mouth. So I thought that if you kept your eyes open and your mouth shut, you weren't likely to come to much harm.

The main source of germs, we reckoned, in our district, was the fever hospital. It was set far away, behind the corporation tip, among green fields and trees. It took a long hot walk to get there, and it was terribly dangerous. Children were taken away and locked up in there, and they never returned. At least, none of my friends had ever returned, to report on its interior. (It never crossed our infant minds that none of our friends had gone there in the first place.)

Being a place of such terror, it was one of constant pilgrimage. We went there at least twice every week. To prove how brave we were. There was a very high blank wall all round it, which we presumed kept the germs in. However, there was a gate and if, as you were passing, that gate was opened, all the germs would come belting out and get you. So, our game was to take a very big breath, shut our mouths tight, nip our noses between finger and thumb and run like hell past the gate.

Only once, while we were passing, the gate opened, horror of horrors, and a nurse came out. She was a plump, pleasant-looking person, who smiled at us. But we knew she must be covered with germs. We redoubled our pace, screaming our heads off (you can scream while you're holding your nose). But I cannoned straight into her. She had a nice cushiony feel, but since she must be covered with germs, I must now be covered with germs. None of my so-called friends would come near me. They trailed behind me, going home, shouting forecasts of my imminent death. I went straight to my money box and gathered up all my savings (tenpence ha'penny) and blued them all on sweets before I died. I was very sick, but I think it was just the enormous number of jelly babies that I swallowed.

Of course, there were other places where germs lurked. Not the toilet, because my mother wiped it out with vast deluges of daily Domestos. I liked nothing better than a good sniff of that incredibly powered life-saving Domestos. I even wondered, if you swallowed enough of it, whether you might become totally germ-proof. Luckily I did not carry out this experiment.

But my mother could do nothing about the grids in the gutters. I would go for a quick peep down them; at the dark-grey steely water that lay within. And beyond, I knew, lay the sewers, where all the germs in the world lurked, waiting to take over the earth. I held my breath as I went past each grid, and nearly died an early death from asphyxiation.

But my first encounter with the nursing profession was far more scary than any mere germ. One day in school there was a queue of bigger lads waiting pale-faced to enter the little room next to the headmaster's office, one by one. I asked what it was for, and my older and more knowledgeable friends cackled evilly and said, 'You'll find out soon enough.' Then somebody whispered the awful words 'Nitty Norah'. And my turn came, soon enough.

Nitty Norah filled the little room; a vast seated mountain of blue and white. Her white front was starched so much it shone and bent like metal. Under her skirt, her thighs looked bigger than the arms on our settee at home. And her hair was steel-grey, and so were the rims of her spectacles, and her eyes were blue and drilled straight through you like machine-gun bullets. Her face was red and ageless, and her hands huge. Her lips were set in a grim line. She said nothing, just gestured with one huge hand for me to approach. Then the great arms reached out, and the huge hands grasped my head, and plunged it straight into her mountainous bosom. I began to choke to death, while the great steely fingers ground their way through my hair.

At last, gasping for air, I was released. She uttered just one word.

'Next.'

I swear I reeled away a broken man. I have never felt the same about women since. In the most romantic moments of my life, when women I loved clutched my head to their bosom, my only thoughts were of near-death, near-extinction, at the hands of Nitty Norah.

I knew in any case I was not long for this world. I had weak kidneys. My mother told me so twice a day. She informed me that I had inherited my weak kidneys from her, for she had weak kidneys as well. When my mother had nothing else to worry about, she worried about my kidneys. Wherever we went, to aunts, grandmas, even on holiday in hotels, whenever the conversation languished, the topic turned to my weak kidneys. Oddly, there were no symptoms, and no cure. You either had weak kidneys or you hadn't. I became a connoisseur of my own urine. Sometimes it was white and sometimes yellow. When it was yellow, was that my kidneys just doing their job, or the beginning of the end? When it was white, was I healthy, or had my kidneys packed up altogether? All I do know is that when my mother finally died at the age of eighty-four, she did not die from weak kidneys. I finally allowed myself to hope . . .

One thing my mother could do much about was my bowels. Her burning question was, 'Have you been yet today?' Other people might worry about Hitler or invasion, but once all our family had been, and she heard the sound of the toilet flushing, my mother felt happily released to go back to worrying about our kidneys. I reckon the sound of the toilet flushing gave my mother as much pleasure as some people get from Handel's *Water Music*.

She had many evil potions to achieve her ends. Senna pods (followed by a rewarding boiled sweet) were not too bad. I think I became a connoisseur of senna pods, rather as some people do of wine. The one I never got used to was Gregory's Powder. This was not soluble, like senna pods. It was a thin sulphurous paste that stuck to your teeth for hours. There is no taste so foul on God's earth as Gregory's Powder mixed with a raspberry-flavoured fruit gum.

On the other hand, I did not mind having boils on my neck. I used to welcome boils on my neck, because my parents seemed to get so much fun out of them. I don't know what happens to boils if they are simply left alone, because my parents were quite unable to leave mine alone. I would sit every evening while hot cloths, wrung out in scalding water, were applied to the back of my neck by my mother. When I had reached the correct stage of parboiledness, my father would move in to squeeze the core out of the wretched boil. The results could be quite spectacular for them, though painful for me. Once I heard them both give squeals of wonder and delight, and my father said, 'Did you see that? It flew right across the room and hit that photo of your Uncle Ernie on the wall!'

You must think by this time I was some kind of masochist. But, you see, for putting up with all this agony, I was given a very splendid Dinky toy. The size of the toy depended on the size of the boil (and, I suppose, whether it hit Uncle Ernie's photo or not). For a small boil, I might only get a tiny lead Spitfire. But for the one that hit Uncle Ernie, I got a complete medium tank set, Royal Tank Regiment. Whenever I felt a boil coming on, I used to whizz straight down to Swan's toyshop, to see what I was going to have next.

Two medical workers I remember with joy. One was Nurse Hall, the town midwife who had delivered me. She was built the same as Nitty Norah, but nice with it. When my mother took me to a whist drive at Nurse Hall's during the war (in the war we mainly seemed to beat Hitler by holding endless whist drives) she loaned me my first 'Just William' book, and they nearly couldn't play whist for the sound of my laughter.

My mother always said, 'I nearly died having you, and you would have died as well, if it hadn't been for Nurse Hall.' All the women swore by her. She'd had seven children herself and knew what it was like. I think that if there'd been an election in the war, and Nurse Hall had stood for parliament, she'd have got in on the female vote alone. She was a heroine of the first water, and her eldest daughter, nearly as big as she was, was her assistant. I only once saw her down. And then the women murmured sympathetically and softly, 'She's had a hard day today. Twenty-eight hours, and she lost them both.'

My other great 'medical' character was Dr Walker. We weren't often ill, any of us, but my father sometimes got influenza and then Dr Walker would come very promptly. And afterwards, my mother would say, 'Cup of tea, Doctor?' and he'd spend half an hour talking to my father. He'd been a doctor in the Indian Army, and was full of exotic tales of snake charmers. He had actually seen the Indian rope-trick performed. He never seemed to be in a hurry: I often wonder about that. My father made sure of Dr Walker's services by paying a couple of shillings off his pay at work every week. It was so simple. Nobody ever complained about not getting enough medical attention. And the people I knew were not the rich, just ordinary working people living on three pounds a week. When I look at all the endless fuss about the National Health Service now, it baffles me.

CHAPTER THIRTEEN

Going Round the Town

I'm dressed up in my Sunday best: tweed belted overcoat the exact replica of my father's; shorts coming just below the knee; shoes my mother's polished till they shine like coal; and the schoolboy cap that's never off my head because it's so useful. For catching butterflies, carrying shells home from the beach, fanning our fire, cleaning blackboards for teacher and, above all, fighting in the schoolyard. Folded, with the hard brim outwards, it's a formidable weapon.

I feel different inside when I put on Sunday best. I expect to feel uncomfortable, know I mustn't run, play tag, climb walls. Once I put my shoes on the wrong feet and never noticed till I got home, because feeling cramped is part of feeling grand, going round the town.

We never set off till dusk, however late that is. Going round the town doesn't work in daylight. It can't start till the lamplighter, a strange silent man whistling under his breath, never talking to us boys because he's in too much of a hurry, has put his ladder against the iron arms of the lamp-posts and lit them.

Round the town is a gaslit world. Naked gas jets flaring inside all the shops and outside, too, at the shopkeeper's expense. Gas jets flaring in the pork-butcher's, against the huge mirrors that cloud and clear as the great clouds of cooking steam hit them. So that at one moment my face, peering in the pork-butcher's window, stares back at me; and next moment it's just a misty blur, creepy as a ghost, so I only know it's me because when I raise my arm it waves back.

The smell of boiling pork, from the seething bath-sized cauldrons, drifts down Saville Street like a hymn in some great cathedral. The pork-shop woman (immensely fat from sampling her own cooking when her back's turned and she thinks no one can see) drips sweat from her pale cheeks and nose as if she was being cooked herself, the biggest pig of all. The whole pigs hanging from sharp steel hooks in the ceiling look slim by comparison. Their skins are scraped as smooth and white as film stars. I reach out and touch one: the skin is horribly like my own, but colder than I ever get, even in winter. I try poking my hand into the long narrow slit where the pig's life once was, and catch the woman watching me in the misted mirror. I pretend to scuff my diamond-bright shoes instead, making half-moons of bare scrubbed planking in the thick sawdust of the floor. But she's too busy to put a hand across my face (which we both know she's perfectly entitled to do, and my father would clout me as well, if he saw her do it). Too busy in her frantic Saturday-night orgy of feeding ten thousand hungry faces coming in for penny-dips (just a bun dipped in the seething cauldron till it's red-hot) or a saveloy-dip (containing a curiously wrinkled sausage), or, best of all, a fourpenny pork sandwich with stuffing. Each is wrapped in a sheet of white paper, dropped as soon as the customer has finished eating it outside. The blizzard of paper spreads out and out from the pork shop as the night goes on, like an early white Christmas. There's no other litter, except the great piles of horse droppings that are spread wider and wider by passing cartwheels, until they're as big and thin as hearthrugs. But the crossing-sweepers are already busy, will be working past midnight, for the streets must be spotless for people going to church tomorrow morning.

Everybody walks and stands in the cobbled street. The only cars belong to rich folk, and are safely away in the garage. There are a few steam lorries parked in side streets, black and gently hissing, with tall chimneys and boilers you can warm your hands against.

Sometimes when you're standing talking, you feel a nudge on your shoulder, and there's a dark-eyed blinkered horse with a lamp-flickering cart behind, waiting to get past.

No room on the pavements. The shop awnings are out, in case it rains, and from them hang chains of two-shilling boots and shoes, ranks of boiler suits and dungarees, and the sad dark overcoats that poor people buy, looking drooping and defeated even before they've begun to fight. (We, grander, buy ours at the Fifty-Shilling Tailors.)

More cheerful are the fruit sellers with their covered barrows and flaring acetylene glowing over a landscape of oranges, apples and tomatoes, a penny a pound.

We push through in single file, my father leading. His head never stops nodding.

'Now, George? What fettle the day, Harry? Hello, Nick, how's the missus?'

Occasionally he turns back to my mother.

'See who that was?'

'No,' says my mother, eyes on some real silk stockings for elevenpence-three-farthings.

'Little Nesser: served me time wi' him at the North-Eastern.'

'Oh, aye,' says my mother, eyes returning to the stockings, her lips moving in silent computation.

Music, every few yards. A man with no legs, sitting on a doorstep, playing a mouth organ, his cap on the pavement beside him, guarded by a small white fox terrier. I stare at where his legs should be; great fat pads of black leather instead. He seems quite happy playing there among a forest of legs. At least he has no legs to stick out and trip up passers-by.

My usual creepy curiosity overcomes me: to dare to get close to him. I ask my father for a ha'penny to put in his cap, one of my Saturday-night privileges. I get it; am mistakenly praised for my soft heart. I run up to him in a flurry, stealing tiny glances at his face, which is fat, lined, very alive. As my ha'penny clinks down he glances up and I flee before he can say anything. If I let him speak, I'd have to admit that he's human. I'd rather think of him as a fabulous beast, like the Headless Woman at the fairground.

A woman plays an accordion, very loud and dramatic, eyes fixed on the chimney pots across the road. Is she mad, or merely blind?

More cheerful, a huge man and his very small wife sing a duet. 'Roses are flowering in Picardy'. If you creep very close, you can hear him mutter to her, with every intake of breath, 'Sing up, you bugger.'

Then we meet somebody we really know. George Lee, sea cook, fresh off his ship, a little capuchin monkey on his shoulder, shivering in a red flannel jacket and helping itself feverishly to peanuts from his breast pocket, cracking them with expert black-leather fingers. The monkey and I stare at each other. It seems much older than me, wiser. Does it know all about Hitler? It sums me up as being of no account, and goes back to frantic nutcracking.

Now we really are stuck for an hour. George will take my father on his latest tour of the world, places like Gib, Rio and Abadan, which sounds like Aberdeen but is in the Gulf. We could even be stuck all night.

'Can I have me pocket money?' My father reaches into his pocket, without stopping listening to how Mussolini's cleaned up the red-light district of Genoa. I have a vision of the great Italian dictator going round with one of my mother's dusters, polishing all the red traffic lights of Italy. My father's hand comes down blindly: in a minute I shall know whether I'm merely rich, or very rich. Depends how much overtime he's worked, or how long he intends standing talking to George Lee.

A shilling! Great! Now I can stand for ages, staring through the window of Swan's toyshop, wondering whether to buy a model of a Fairey Battle bomber, or a Glasgow Corporation Tram, or save it towards the Royal Tank Corps light tank set.

In half an hour I'm back to find the monkey gone, replaced by my cousin Ada. My father has just fatally asked Ada how her mam is. Ada will now spend an hour giving us every symptom of every member of her family since we last saw her, which is only once a year, thank God.

Off to the little narrow tobacconist that sells hot sarsaparilla by the glass. You drink it sitting in his narrow mahogany booths with prickly worn-leather seats, looking at the bits of your face showing up in his mirrors, cut into fragments by painted advertisements for Gold Flake and Capstan Navy Cut. Great talker, this tobacconist, with his bald head, gold spectacles and long brown coat. He calls me 'my little man' and asks my opinion of the Polish Corridor and the latest Torso Murder Case. I have to hold my end up, because he knows my father, and tells him all the quaint and amusing replies I make.

It's all dead safe really. Because everyone knows my father, or at least Nana, and has seen me in my pram when I was little and knew my aunt Rose when she was a girl in the last war and went on route marches with the soldiers and carried their rifles when they got tired.

The town is filling up now, you can hardly move. The cinemas must be out, the Rex, Albion, Princes, Boro', Howard Hall, Comedy and Carlton. The pubs, too, because there's Granda, grand in waistcoat, watch and gold Albert. He carries his skinful magnificently, only has a slight tendency to sing, which Nana stamps on firmly.

And so to bed.

But not to sleep.

I can't sleep because there's a torch and three large toy pistols under my pillow and they keep working down under my shoulders. Is there going to be a war? That's why the torch and pistols are there. I think about the Germans: the situation is perfectly simple.

The Germans are the bullies of the European classroom. Lots of little countries have been getting their arms twisted behind their backs. But in the corner of that classroom, Britain is sitting, best fighter in the school, captain of football, popular hero. Britain has got her feet up on the window sill at present, reading a book, because the bully hasn't gone too far. Yet! But when the little kids squeal too loud, Britain will get up and give the bully a bloody nose.

The bully will crumple up, snivelling snots in the corner, and then we'll have peace.

Simple. Happened before, in 1918. Look at the map: half the world is coloured red, for British. Germany is a pathetic little green postage stamp; there is hardly room to print the word 'Berlin'.

I have one or two doubts. My father says the Germans are good engineers; he will buy me German toys, the rest are 'foreign rubbish'. My father respects German gunnery, after the Battle of Jutland, in the Last Lot. German captains keep clean ships: when they are in port, all their sailors march to the Seamen's Mission to worship in immaculate uniforms. The Germans, unlike the Latin races, are 'clean-living' men.

My mother is mortally afraid the U-boats will starve Britain to death. In the Last Lot she queued for four hours for a piece of suet but when she got to the front, it had all gone. But U-boats are just another example of sneaky German cowardice, attacking unarmed merchant ships: when our destroyers get there, they always depth-charge them into soup!

German bombers have evil names like Dornier and Heinkel and Stuka. They have evil shapes, long, thin and pointed, like snakes and dragons, praying mantises and stingrays. They are always painted black and carry the crooked cross. They only bomb women and children.

British aeroplanes are honest brown and green, and look like faithful dogs with friendly names like Hurricane and Wellington and Hampden.

Suddenly I am stricken with doubts. Will our faithful dogs be able to cope with the poisonous dragons? Then I remember about the Supermarine Spitfire. I don't know anything about the Spitfire. I've only seen it on a cigarette card, and the artist didn't know much about the Spitfire either, because he's painted it coming out of the sun, with no details. But that Spitfire is black too, and looks even more shark-like and poisonous than the Germans'.

Reassured, I remember about 'ersatz'. Everything the Germans have is 'ersatz'. They make 'ersatz' coffee by stealing acorns off their pigs and roasting them, and it tastes 'yuk', but they can't afford real coffee. Their soldiers' boots have 'ersatz' cardboard soles that fall apart as soon as it rains. They're trying to make petrol out of potatoes because they haven't got any oil. (That's why they still pull their field guns with horses.) All the oil and tin and rubber in the world comes from Malaya, which is part of the great British Empire. If a war comes, our Navy will starve them out. Like in the Last Lot.

And the Germans have the hopeless burden of Hitler: a total nutter. If he can't get his own way, he falls down foaming at the mouth and chews the carpet. Every kid you meet is pulling a lock of hair down over his forehead, sticking his finger under his nose and screaming fake German till his throat conks out or somebody kicks him. We do the goose-step till we fall over laughing. And there are songs:

> Ven der Führer says
> Ve iss der Master Race,
> Ve vart, vart,
> Right in der Führer's face.

Too many *bravissimo* performances of this epic have greatly increased our mothers' burden of underpants' washing. Then that other song, to the tune of Colonel Bogey:

Adolf . . . has only got one ball
Goering . . . he has none at all . . .

(We would be enthralled, in 1945, when a Russian post-mortem on the Führer's body actually proved the first line to be true. We waited with avidity for the disappointing results of the inquest on Goering.)

So, did I want a war? Well, I'd spent a long time collecting two sets of cigarette cards: 'Air-raid precautions' and 'Aircraft of the RAF'. And I didn't want to have wasted my time. I didn't want to waste the lovely Spitfires either. And the goodies always won: every film and book said so.

Yes, I wanted a war.

Mind made up, I rolled over and slept.

CHAPTER FOURTEEN

A State of War

Mr Chamberlain's broadcast was not impressive. I remembered him from the newsreels, coming out of his aeroplane after Munich, waving his little piece of paper and promising 'peace in our time'. I thought he looked like a sheep, and now he bleated like a sheep. He 'regretted' that a state of war now existed between Great Britain and Germany. He sounded really hurt, like Hitler was some shiftless council tenant who had failed to pay his rent after faithfully promising to do so.

That wasn't the way to talk to Hitler. He should be threatening to kick his teeth in; I knew there'd be trouble.

There was. The sirens went immediately. We didn't know what to do. We had no shelters, nothing but little gas masks in cardboard boxes. But at least we had the gas masks; even babies and horses. Babies' gas masks were as big as those for horses, but the whole baby went inside, and the baby's mother played a sort of concertina-thing to give the baby air. Little kids had blue and red gas masks that looked like Mickey Mouse, to cheer them up, but I had a grown-up black one, like my mother and father.

We went to the front windows and stared out. Everything was peaceful and sunny. My mother didn't know what to do about our roast Sunday dinner. My father said to turn the gas off, in case the oven got hit by a bomb. The only defence in sight was old Charlie Brown, famous for his bad chest from the trenches of the last war, and his consumption of Newcastle Brown ale. Charlie had volunteered to be an air-raid warden the day before. He wanted to do his bit, but he didn't know what his bit was. He marched stiffly round and round the green like the smart soldier he had once been, in his best Sunday suit with his gas mask in a little cardboard box hung from his shoulders on a piece of string.

'If he sounds his rattle,' said my father, 'put on your gas mask quick.'

'He hasn't got a rattle,' I said.

The world seemed broken in half. The earth, the houses, roses, sunlit trees were still England. But the air was suddenly German: there wasn't a Spitfire or a Hurricane, or even a Gloster Gladiator in sight. Soon, like on the newsreels from Spain, the air would fill with the orderly black crosses of German bombers, with endless strings of tiny bombs falling from their bellies. And only Charlie Brown to stop them. I'd accumulated a tin of sweets to eat in the air-raid shelter during air raids. Except we hadn't got a shelter. It was all lying in bits of corrugated iron on our front lawn, where the council workmen had dumped it yesterday. The corrugations were full of water, and little birds were having a bath in them.

I couldn't stand still: I went into my bedroom and considered trying to pray, a thing I hadn't done for years. It didn't seem much use against Nazi bombers. The Spaniards must have been great prayers, being Catholics, and it hadn't done them much good.

My old teddy bear was sitting in the corner. I hadn't spared him a glance in years either, but now he looked at me appealingly. I put him under the bed for safety.

Then the all-clear sounded.

Charlie Brown headed straight for the Cannon Inn and downed several pints double-quick.

We put up our shelter the following Saturday afternoon. Everybody was out digging their big holes, like square graves, in their back gardens. It was like an archaeology party. I was in charge of counting nuts and bolts, and also rescuing the bemused worms that wriggled out of the straight sides of the hole. And making a collection of blackened pennies, with the old Queen's head on them, and bits of clay pipe that my father's spade turned up. And keeping up a steady gun duel, with my largest toy pistol, at Brian Spedding who was dug in two holes away. I slept with it, and my torch, under my pillow, awakening most mornings with it digging into my cheekbone, leaving a red mark that lasted until lunchtime. My mother tried to make me stop it, but I told her that we all had to suffer for the War Effort.

We were two feet six down when my father's spade struck on a long earthenware pipe running across the bottom of the hole. The neighbours gathered round, and announced it was a field drain from the old farm. If we broke into it, the water from the whole field would fill our shelter every time it rained. So we stopped there, and put up the curving silvery sides of the shelter, me doling out the nuts and bolts carefully, because there was a War On. By evening, with the earth piled back on top, we had a place to run to.

And over the next weeks, much more. A little palace; a home from home. My father painted the walls white, and threw handfuls of tiny bits of cork that stuck into the wet paint. These, he said, would absorb the moisture of our breath on freezing nights. A floor of old second-hand doors, and then bits of unwanted floral carpet. Then a neat wooden front door for the shelter to keep out the draughts, and a porch of sandbags to keep out the rain. Second-hand wooden armchairs, and an electric cable that led from the house to work the light and fire. I think he would have hung pictures of ships on the walls, if they hadn't been curved.

The end of the little palace came when a warden came round inspecting the shelters. The palace was pronounced a death trap. If a bomb burst nearby, our lovely little front door would explode into shards of wood, spearing our flesh. The severed electric-light cable would touch the steel walls of the shelter and fry us alive. And, above all, the shelter was not dug deep enough. In vain my father pleaded the field drain. Dig deeper or lose your shelter, said the man from the ARP.

My father dismantled and dug deeper. The moment he'd finished, it rained. The shelter filled a foot deep with water. My father built a precarious floor of wooden doors above the flood, with a trapdoor for bailing out. The shelter became merely a well, used for watering the chrysanthemums in the greenhouse.

The government responded by sending two workmen to move our shelter from the back garden to the front, clear of the field drain. We had bunks, but no mattresses, so that the iron springs left curious red tartan marks on your hip in the morning. Our light was a three-inch paraffin lamp, a present from Scarborough never meant for serious use, with a little glass shade. Our heater was one candle under a large plant pot: the plant pot was a little warmer than the rest of the shelter, if you put your hands on it.

We now shared our shelter with the Speddings, Brian and me on the bottom bunks, and my mother and Mrs Spedding dangling their legs above. I became aware of the charms of the female leg. My mother had slim ladylike legs in pinkish rayon stockings: Mrs Spedding's legs were altogether more provocative, in a gingery shade.

They cancelled school immediately 'for the duration of the Emergency'. Handy, as I had a lot to do. There was the map of Europe, given away free with the first copy of *War Weekly* to pin on my bedroom wall; lots of little flags to cut: British, French, German and, bafflingly, Russian. I also hung up score charts for German ships sunk, planes shot down, tanks destroyed.

Then Stanley and I set off on our bikes to look for the War. Somebody said they were desperate for people to fill sandbags at Preston Hospital, to protect the windows, so we dashed down there. Unfortunately, the hospital porter turned out to be old Jack Dawson, our bossy neighbour. He turned us back at the gate, saying he didn't want a lot of kids hanging about the place. We considered reporting him to the police, for sabotaging the War Effort.

We worked out ways of fooling German bombers. If they machine-gunned us from the air, we'd pretend to fall down dead, then get up and run again, then pretend to die again. This would ruin their estimate of civilian casualties.

We lived on our bikes, looking for Defences, which seemed in perilously short supply. Every little bit of barbed wire went down in our notebooks, even the thin strands round farmers' fields, which didn't really count but we put them down just the same. Then real Defences appeared: single pom-poms on the Bank Top; armed trawlers. We inspected them daily, looking for improvements, and making sure the crews knew their job. Best were the barrage balloons. We spent hours at

Dockwray Square, staring through the railings. The balloon was like a great silver elephant, whose sides crinkled with every breeze. In the evenings, the RAF crew played football with us, till the girls came and they lost all interest in football. We thought of reporting them to the police, for neglecting the War Effort. Playing football with us kept them fit, but daft giggling girls were sure to ruin their morale.

Bob (1939)

Then they restarted school, mornings only. We still couldn't actually go to school, because they hadn't built its air-raid shelters yet. Our class, only, met in the old winding-house of Preston Colliery, a huge dank brick underground arch that smelt evilly of cats. That winding-house was our air-raid shelter. Later in the war, it sustained a near miss from a very small bomb and collapsed, killing forty. On fine days, we wandered round the town in a crocodile, looking for a place to sit down together. We usually ended up in Preston Cemetery, sitting on the tombstones, doing sums. Stanley reckoned this was so that if there was an air raid, and we got killed by bombs, we could be buried immediately, without being taken home first.

It was becoming increasingly hard to find any way of beating Hitler. We even volunteered to help knit comforts for the troops. We would hold the hanks of wool before us, on outstretched hands, while the girls wound it into balls. They were very bossy, constantly shouting at us, 'Hold your hands up, can't you?' Then the vicar's wife got sarky about the quality of our mothers' knitting, announcing, 'We are trying to knit comforts for the troops, my dears, not discomforts.' So most of the mothers gave it up in a huff. My mother gave me her balaclava helmet instead.

My father joined the wardens. They had one interesting night in our square, practising putting out real incendiary

Outbreak of war (1939) and Bob's father as an ARP Warden (on the right), his mother and the neighbours

bombs with sand. They had to summon the ambulance; the wardens were so enthusiastic, everyone got their eyes full of sand, and they took the bomb-fins away so we couldn't have them for souvenirs. All that the wardens did otherwise was hold a Saturday-night whist drive and dance for their funds. I was put in charge of lemonade-selling. I sold an incredible amount of lemonade, ginger pop and American ice-cream soda; I learnt to play whist and won the booby prize, and I learnt ballroom dancing. But it didn't seem to have a lot to do with beating Hitler.

Perhaps Hitler was already beaten. The German pocket-battleship *Graf Spee* ran away from three very small British cruisers, and scuttled herself in Montevideo harbour, though she had suffered little damage except a shell in her bakery. The German captain said his crew could not fight on without a supply of fresh bread, and shot himself. To us kids, if the Germans were all like the crew of the *Graf Spee*, there didn't seem a lot to beat.

The first raid came as we were sitting down to dinner. When the sirens went we left everything and ran to the shelter. I sat at the shelter door and stared at the sunlit path only inches from my nose, thinking, 'In here it's safe, but out there is Danger.' I couldn't resist putting a finger out into Danger, like it was a bowl of hot water. Nothing happened, so I put my whole hand out, whereupon my mother clouted me for mucking about. I saw a beetle crawling on the path, in Danger. It seemed quite unworried. I imagined a huge piece of shrapnel coming down and squashing it flat. But the beetle would never know it was in Danger, and it still wouldn't know when it was squashed flat. So for the beetle, war didn't exist. And the birds were singing as well, and I felt stupid cowering in this hole, and wondered why wars were only for People.

Then my mother started worrying about the meal getting cold on the table, and fretting that the dog might eat it. So she nipped out and fetched the sausage and chips and we ate them. Then she went back for the bread and butter, and finally the prunes and custard, and then to make a cup of tea. The whole shelter was full of dirty plates and it was embarrassing because Mrs Spedding and Brian hadn't had their dinner yet, and there wasn't enough for them. But my mother gave them a cup of tea.

My mother was just thinking about nipping out to do the washing up, and worrying about her two o'clock appointment at the hairdresser's, when the guns started, out to sea. The sound got nearer, like thunder, then worse than thunder. Like the sky was cracking in half.

Then we heard people shouting. Not screaming, but shouting like a football crowd, only scattered over the whole district. The people in the next shelter were outside, so I nipped out, and there was the German bomber streaking up the river, so long and thin you could tell it was a Dornier Flying Pencil. And bursts of anti-aircraft fire, like grey balls of cotton wool growing in the sky, in clumps of four, miles behind the bomber.

The man next door was jumping up and down on top of his shelter, screaming his head off. 'Get yer eyes chaarked, ye stupid buggers,' he was shouting at the gunners. 'What ye think ye're paid for?'

'Mind yer language in front o' that bairn, Jack!' said his wife, but he took no notice.

When the gunners missed again, you could hear the whole

district groaning like a football crowd. The man next door began pulling his plants up, he was so mad. Then when there was another set of bangs he would look up and cover up his eyes, saying he couldn't bear to look.

Just as the bomber seemed to be getting away, it flew right into a cluster of grey cotton wool, and came out the other side as a mass of bits. You should have heard the cheering. Like Newcastle United had scored the winning goal for the FA Cup. It echoed and echoed.

Then the man next door said, 'They were brave lads for Germans. They flew in a straight line and didn't run away.' There were tears in his eyes. And everybody else began saying how brave the German airmen had been, but why did they dare to fly so low, straight and slow?

Because they were photographing the ships in the river, said someone else.

We are really for it now.

PART TWO

1940–1948 War, Peace and Tynemouth High School

CHAPTER FIFTEEN

The Battle for Britain

Things went so quickly and disastrously wrong in the spring of 1940 that it can only be likened to a test match against Australia. One minute we were mining Norwegian territorial waters to stop German iron-ore ships creeping cringingly down in terror of the Royal Navy. And the next, France had fallen.

There was a sort of tingle in the air when I got up one morning; a sinking feeling in the gut, if you thought too much about it, and yet a heady excitement as well. Our radio was on all day, and they kept playing a fierce trumpet record, called 'The Trumpet Voluntary', between the announcements. Whoever thought of that was a genius: it keyed you up. I'd never realized why armies used trumpets before. It was harsh and bitter, and made you feel braver.

I couldn't understand why the French had surrendered. According to my war map, they still had nine-tenths of their country left. In the Last Lot, the Germans had nearly got to Paris, had bombarded the city with huge guns like Big Bertha, and the French hadn't given in, and had won in the end. What was the matter with them now?

Of course, they had old-fashioned weapons. Daft old-fashioned helmets with a ridge along the top, and pale-blue uniforms and puttees the same as in the last war, instead of our new battledress. Their bombers tended to have three engines, their fighters were always ten miles slower than ours, their tanks had absurd round turrets and their submarines had huge guns instead of sensible torpedoes. But that was no reason for giving up.

I went for a walk, I was so worried. I met a kid on a building site who said the French had only pretended to surrender; they'd waved a white flag, and when the Germans got out of their trenches, the French had shot them down like dogs. This was the first sensible suggestion I'd heard all day. I ran home to tell my father the good news. He was not impressed.

People kept saying the French were decadent. Hints of black underwear and too much ooh-la-la in Paris. Till somebody said 'not in front of the child'. My mother thought that a lack of decent flush toilets had sapped their morale. They drank wine instead of tea, every day! My father was pretty quiet. He said that the French had stood up to Jerry well in the Last Lot. Then Mr Churchill broadcast and said, 'The Battle of France is over: the Battle of Britain is about to begin.'

I felt better and went out on my bike to look for signs of the Battle of Britain.

It started eventually with the sound of aeroplanes. It was a warm, muggy, overcast day, and raining. We looked out of the classroom window, and couldn't see a thing. We didn't recognize the zhoooorzh, zhoooorzh, zhoooorzh of unsynchronized German aircraft engines in those days.

Then there was the sound of a boy running a stick along a set of iron railings, far away. More boys running sticks along iron railings. Then the sound of aeroplanes went really wild, like they were going to crash above the clouds.

Then the sirens went. We had to run to the surface brick

shelter down the street. A sloping wet, slippery street, and all the time the sound of invisible aeroplanes going mad just above us.

Then a Spitfire came diving down through the clouds, vertically, just above us. We thought it was going to crash on us, but it pulled out just above the rooftops, and flew round and round in circles, as if it was frightened a German had followed it. Then it put its nose up and disappeared back into the clouds as vertically as it had come down.

Nobody was looking where they were going. Someone stumbled and we all fell over him, and we all arrived in a heap at the door of the shelter and crawled inside for the noise of the invisible aeroplanes was deafening. We kept on trying to nip out again to have a quick look: the teacher had to clout one or two for it.

When the all-clear sounded we were sent home. The streets were covered with little heavy silver mushrooms: bullets that had flattened themselves as they had hit the ground. You could still find them months afterwards, hidden under the privet hedges.

The news said that seventeen German raiders had been shot down, but that the battle had taken place over the Farne Islands, about forty miles north of us.

Then came the night raids, the real Blitz. Night after night after night. Was I frightened? No, not really. I was scared when I heard bombs falling, and knew they were near. You listened to the scream of them, rising in pitch as they grew nearer and nearer, and you counted to ten. If you reached ten, still counting, the bomb had missed you and you were still alive. The bunk you were lying on would kick you, there would be a rumble of falling bricks, and a patter of wood and stones on the soil over your head, and everybody would start breathing again and say, 'That was a close one!'

'Verne Road?'

'The Quadrant.'

But in the morning, when you climbed out of the shelter and looked for gaps in the houses, the gaps were always further away than you thought. Our skyline at the Green never changed in the whole war.

You were not afraid because you were part of a team. Playing for England. Everybody was in the team. Being brave and silent while a bomb was dropping made you at one with the soldiers and the sailors and the airmen. Getting dressed at three in the morning in pitch darkness and going down to the shelter in the freezing cold was giving old Hitler a poke in the eye. And like a good team, we cared about each other: every baby, every granny was part of us. People called from shelter to shelter, passing on the most fantastic rumours that grew and grew, but they caused no panic, they just made you feel solemn, like being in church. You were a tiny part of some great thing. For the only time in my life I felt part of the whole world and part of history. And it made you feel safe, whether you lived or died. If you died, you would automatically become a hero, whispered about, and remembered. One, in the waiting rooms to heaven, with destroyer captains and fighter pilots, and who could ask for greater company? It is not death that makes you feel unsafe, but people breaking the rules, like terrorists.

As I have said, when war broke out my father became a section leader in the wardens. In his day job he wore a filthy boiler suit, but as a warden a clean one. Other wardens clustered round him as he walked, just like the workmen.

The wardens were wonderful, going from shelter to shelter, giving news, turning the chaos of bangs and flashes into hard common sense. My father seemed to know more about the raids than anybody else. He'd come home from work and say, 'There's still a yellow alert on. The buggers is hanging around somewhere.' He knew where raids had taken place; where they'd been bad; where an enemy bomber had been shot down. He always gave the impression of being in good control of the situation. He never used dramatic words like 'Hun' or 'Nazi': always 'them buggers', said in the same tone of voice he might use about a stroppy Irish boilermaker, or the Nigerian labourer who always went for a snooze in the heat of the retort house.

They came for him at any hour of the day or night. When he was at home, my mother dreaded the knock on the door, the anxious black-capped figure with the inevitable question, 'Is Bobby in?' Sometimes, when he had dropped asleep in a chair, exhausted, she used to tell them he'd gone out. But he always slept with one ear cocked, and she was always pulled up in the middle of her lies by his call of, 'Who's there, Maggie?'

During raids he toured his district, talking to the people in the shelters. He always believed in telling people what was going on. Anything was better than the chaotic series of thuds, bangs, crumps, whistlings and hisses that was an air raid. Women used to stop my mother in the street and thank her for my father 'keeping an eye on them'.

He seemed to go through air raids with the wonder and gusto of a small boy. He would talk of the weird beauty of the 'chandeliers', the marvellous cages of blue lights that dropped slowly by parachute, lighting the target for the

German bombers, and he liked it even better when the ack-ack gunners blew them to bits. One night he heard the soft whispering of a cluster of incendiaries coming down straight above his head. He just managed to get under a coster-monger's barrow before they hit. Then there was a ring of them burning around him, and several burning through the barrow on top of him, and he thought his last moment had come. He escaped by taking a flying kick at one of them, to make a gap to run through.

'Scored a goal, an' all!'

All night we listened for his footsteps, the clink of hobnailed warden's boots. Mostly they'd walk steadily, even when German bombers were overhead. But sometimes they'd start to run, and then we'd hear the whistle of the bombs. He'd come through the shelter door-curtain in a flying leap, and land on his knees between the bunks with a shelter-shaking thud. Then he'd sit up and say, 'By, I could do wi' a drop o' coffee, hinny.'

My mother only worried when he was on night shift at the gasworks. Climbing the ladders of the great gasholder to kick burning incendiaries off the thin top plates. Chipping ice off a conveyor a hundred feet up, with an air raid in progress. All he would say is, 'I'm all right. I know those old works better than bloody Hitler.' He seemed to love it all. My dearest ambition was to reach the age of fifteen and be his official ARP messenger. Sadly, the end of war beat me to it.

Of course we grew weary when there were three air-raid warnings in one night. Little kids cried at being woken for the third time and taken out into the frost; blankets that had been neatly folded the first time were trailing on the wet ground by the end. And all for single bombers, sent at hourly intervals, simply to disturb the workers' sleep, because Hitler could afford nothing more.

It was then that I did know terror. I fell asleep for the third time in the shelter, to the sound of the others' heavy breathing, the flicker of the little oil lamp, the strange searchlight glow that the candle in the plant pot cast on the curving ceiling.

I wakened in total darkness. No glow of oil lamp or candle. No sound of breathing from above me or across the gangway where the Speddings lay. Not even a dark-blue edge round the curtain that covered the shelter door. It was like being in a cold black tomb.

I thought, a bomb has dropped while I've been asleep, and killed the others and buried me alive. For a moment I froze in panic, then I rolled out of my bunk on to the floor of the shelter, which should have been six inches below.

I fell, not six inches, but two feet. I screamed my head off. The world had gone mad. Then the room was flooded with electric light, and I saw my mother standing in her nightdress, with her hand on the switch. I was in my own bedroom in the house. That last time I had walked from the shelter in my sleep and got undressed and got into bed, without ever waking up.

My mother was always very calm: I only saw her go to pieces once.

I wakened one winter night with a sense of something terribly wrong. The light was on in the sitting room and I could hear my mother wailing.

'Eeh, Bob, I wish you would come, I wish you would come.' My father was on night shift. I could also hear the dog howling. Hitler had got us at last.

I ran out in my pyjamas. My mother was standing in the middle of the kitchen, wearing a raincoat over her nightdress, and holding an umbrella over her head. The kitchen was full of sparkling, falling rain, glinting in the lamplight. The dog was standing faithfully beside her, soaking wet and shaking himself every two minutes. The kitchen floor was an inch under water.

I could think of nothing to do but stand beside her. She turned to me and said, 'Put your coat on, or you'll catch your death.'

And there we stood, paralysed, looking at the burst water pipe like sun-worshippers stare at the sun, until our upstairs neighbour, old Jack Dawson, suddenly appeared in response to my mother's wails, seized a huge hammer and beat the water pipe flat with three blows of terrible violence.

The sparkling rain stopped. My mother came out of her paralysis.

'Thank you, Jack. Could you do with a cup of tea?' And she began, like a mended toy, to sweep the water out of the kitchen with a broom.

To listen to her, the only important thing about the war was getting enough cigarettes for my father. My father never sat still between 1939 and 1945. All that kept him going were twenty full-strength Capstan a day. Without nicotine, he was like a Spitfire without petrol. Some of his mates would call at the shop on their way to work. If the shop had cigarettes, they'd go on to work; if not, they'd go back to bed.

So crisis point for my mother was Friday afternoons, when she walked round the whole town looking for cigarettes. She was pretty and had a lot of charm, all of which was used on the tobacconists. It used to outrage me: we'd be walking round the town in the rain, and she'd be giving me stick because she was fed up, and then at the tobacconist's door she'd turn on the charm like a searchlight. I once called her a hypocrite, and nearly got a clout.

Worst were the shops that had only Turkish cigarettes. You'd see a horrible little hand-lettered sign in the shop window: 'Pashas only.' My father said Pashas were made from camel dung. But they were better than nothing. Only, if she was offered them early on she didn't know what to do. If she bought Pashas, she wouldn't be able to afford better cigarettes further on round the town.

When we got to my grandmother's for tea, my father would have got there from work. He'd be smoking half-inch dog-ends, burning his nose with the match as he lit them. Or just sitting there panting. My mother would always play a trick on him, getting any Pashas out of her shopping bag first and then watching his face fall. Then she'd bury the Pashas with Gold Flake and Players, and every packet she pulled out, his face would light up more. And her face used to look so proud, as if she'd presented him with a bouncing baby boy.

During the war, a woman's most prized possession was a pair of fur-lined boots. Unobtainable in the shops, with or without clothing coupons. But one day my father met a chap who had two pairs for sale. They were my mother's size. My mother asked what colour they were: my father hadn't bothered to ask. My mother had a very subtle taste in colour: my father's taste could only be described as 'garish'.

That night he brought home a superb pair of boots which were quite the foulest shade of acid-green that I had ever seen. My mother stared at them in agony.

'I thought they looked bonny,' said my father.

Silence.

'They'll mucky-down, given time.'

Silence.

'Well, they'll keep your feet warm, anyway.'

Silence.

'I'd have got the other pair, only they were a dull brown.'

My mother weighed the boots in her hand and contemplated my father's head. Then, 'They're lovely,' she said, with a smile of pure agony.

Eventually, our school was flattened by a landmine, and also the Rex Cinema next door. The Rex manager, a good bloke who told us jokes and made us laugh at Saturday-morning matinées, was killed outright. Both the headmaster and the nastiest teacher in the school, Miss Townsend, were buried for hours in the wreckage, but dug out unharmed. We were outraged. We all wished they'd been killed, instead of the Rex manager, because they were both terrible caners and complete Nazi sadists. Miss Townsend actually had blonde hair coiled in plaits round her head and thick muscular legs just like the Hitler Youth Madchen. My mother wondered what they'd been up to, fire-watching in the school on their own.

Unfortunately we were transferred to Spring Gardens School immediately, all classes having to sit together in the hall, with the Spring Gardens kids peering in at us and laughing, like we were something in the zoo.

Stanley was evacuated to Hexham, but returned after a fortnight. Some Hexham kids pushed him backwards into a cowpat. The woman he was billeted with didn't wash his blazer, and he had to go to school with the dry cowpat stuck to him, and she didn't clean his shoes or make his bed or anything. And the teacher kept remarking how scruffy town kids were. So he came home: he said it was all cows and cowpats and boring.

CHAPTER SIXTEEN

Grandfather Westall

Sunday lunch, 1941. Waiting for grandfather to come home from the pub. Granda and Nana have been bombed out and are living with us. There are a few frictions: I have to sleep on the front-room couch, among the dark funereal furniture and the incense of mothballs. My mother is left-handed and my grandmother right-handed, so as each goes to pick up the poker to stoke the fire alternately they keep on picking up the black end instead of the handle, but all this pales by comparison with Sunday lunch.

The pub shuts at two. It will take Granda seventeen minutes to meander through the streets to our house and he will arrive prompt at 2.17. But my mother has always put lunch on the table at 1.30 and shows no sign of changing her ways. So, after a steamy Sunday morning of pans boiling on the hob in the living room, sending the occasional snake of foam darting down their sides to hiss to death on the glowing coals, the whole roast lunch sits being shrivelled to mummification in the oven. The smell fills the house and is marvellous. The smell of it is all we will enjoy. Meanwhile the atmosphere thickens like a thunderstorm. My father tries to pretend to read the paper. I try to read the paper; every crackle of newsprint is like a sudden brattle of thunder. Nobody can shift a leg to ease it without the rest noticing. My mother says at steady intervals that the lunch is being ruined.

Once would be understandable, I think to myself. But every week? It's like the return of the Prodigal Son in church, only the fatted calf is reduced to a cinder before the Prodigal arrives. Why don't they just change the time? Why is Granda awaited with such massive disapproval? Only Nana sits calmly, hands in her lap, blue eyes comfortably dreaming, far away.

Certainly, when the Prodigal arrives, he doesn't seem very terrible. He is respectably dressed in a dark-blue suit with a waistcoat, and a check cap, with his silver watch and chain drooping from his waistcoat in two grand loops. He is not visibly drunk. He may hum a song to himself, but he doesn't stagger or seem in any danger of throwing up. But the smell of beer from his breath mingles sickly with the incense of shrivelling meat. And that smell, I have been taught, is the smell of the pit itself.

Lunch is a silent meal. When my mother serves it, the serving spoons ring savagely on the plates like an executioner's axe. She hits the plate over and over again, to shake the last shred of pea or potato and turnip on to the plate, and in every stroke is her rage. The only words are furtive offers of second helpings. Sometimes my grandfather will push away his plate from him, the meal half eaten, as a kind of mute savage protest. I don't blame him, I can hardly eat myself, my stomach is so curdled, and I am not the target of all this wrath. Sometimes my mother or father will also push their plates away, half eaten, in a gesture of retaliatory disgust: it is very deep, this gesture of refusing to eat with each other. I don't dare do it. Nana sensibly finishes her meal.

But what has Granda done to be in such disgrace?

Granda is the wreck of a monster. A docker by trade, though as I give him a sideways glance, he seems to have all the moustached dignity and authority of Lord Haig in the recruiting posters. But before the last war, the Great War, he was different. Family legend says he was a man of great stubborn endurance. He found a place in South Shields where he worked, across the river, where he could buy a bag of coal threepence cheaper than on our north side. So, every Saturday after work, he went and bought a sack and carried it a mile to the ferry. At the ferry he hit a snag. If he put the sack down on the deck to rest, he would be charged an extra penny by the ferryman for luggage. But if he kept the sack on his back all the way, that is 'personal possessions' and he would be charged nothing. So every Saturday night he walked aboard with his ticket between his teeth and the sack on his back, standing out the voyage, sweat on his brow and his arms cracking, and the ferryman watching him every inch of the way. But he watched in vain: the sack never touched the deck. Then Granda walked off and walked the other mile home. Then he would spend ten shillings on beer. And when he was in drink on Saturday nights my father and Nana used to go and hide in the wash house when they heard his step, and stay there, silent as mice until he collapsed into drunken insensibility on the horsehair sofa. Then Nana would rifle his pockets of whatever remained of his pay, and she would go and pay the week's rent and spend every last penny on food in the late-opening shops. And when he wakened he would rage against the pickpocket who had stolen his money on the way home from the pub. He never seemed to wonder who paid the rent or where the food came from. But Nana always left him enough money for one drink. After that, the magnificent silver watch and chain would go to the pawnshop, until he redeemed it the next pay day.

But the Great War did for him. He volunteered at forty in 1914, giving a false age. He gave me one bit of advice from that time. The moment you are off duty, go to bed. Because when they come round looking for men for fatigues, they take the men sitting dressed playing cards.

I don't know if it was gas, or merely bronchitis from the wet earth of the trenches, but he came back with a bad chest that knocked all the giant strength out of him. He seemed to spend half his life in bed coughing: for the rest, he was a silent man. When we were in company, I regarded him with respectful distant awe. Our real salvation together came via his 'box of bits', a tea chest filled with the most incredible collection of household junk I have ever known. Brass taps, green with verdigris, entangled in yards of wire in which were also caught shoe trees, bayonet handles, miniature brass pans made by apprentices as test pieces in the shipyards. You grabbed an end of wire and pulled, and each time a new random string of objects emerged from the chest. Oh, the joy of disentangling, sorting, arranging and finding out the history of everything. For on the contents of his own tea chest, Granda was a true expert historian; where they'd come from, who gave them to him, when and why. I think we travelled as far as Borneo, and well back into the nineteenth century. Each item would start off a stream of memory, and I was content to sit and listen. At five, I became an historian, an antique collector, a social observer. He, living again his tormented life, must have found a little ease. I like to think so: it was the only converse we ever had.

I think my father understood; he never said so, but he would sometimes join in the reminiscences. To Nana, they were just the bairn playing, and let him be if he's happy. She would cheerfully have picked her way through the junk all day to keep me happy. To my mother, it was a disgraceful chaos, to be cleared away as old rubbish as soon as possible.

I valued him; he was a source of deep mystery, a monster, a fabulous beast who might be approached in fear and trembling. I think I first came to a sense of the mystery of the death of the body through him. He was always in danger of dying. When he was poorly, I would go and see him with my father (having nothing to say to him, as usual) and I would stare in fascination at the blackness inside his mouth and the blackness inside his hairy nostrils. It worried me more that people said I was like him. Even beloved Nana said that. Like him in being big and broad when my parents were quite small. His eyes were too close together, they said, and so were mine. Eyes being too close together was considered a certain sign of evil nature when I was young, but the characteristic seems to have gone out of fashion. I used to wonder if I was like him. Whether I had untapped sources of drunken violence in me and whether I would one day throw a cast-iron gas stove down the stairs.

But in the end I accepted the possibility philosophically. He might be a monster but he wasn't a ghost. And he was quite an original and spectacular monster. I wouldn't mind, really. I already had a taste for being talked about, and a dreadful fear of being dull and boring. Whatever Granda was, he wasn't boring.

CHAPTER SEVENTEEN

The Spectre of Specky-Four-Eyes

Tynemouth High School, which I reached at the age of eleven in the autumn of 1941, was the Kingdom of Heaven. Oak-panelled walls, masters in swirling black gowns, a huge library and, best of all, the great honour boards on the walls, stretching back into the remote past of the nineteenth century and stretching forward so that my own name might one day appear on them. Above all, learning for learning's sake. I began to learn about some incredibly ancient people who lived in Ur of the Chaldees, six thousand years ago. What they ate, how they built their houses, how they transported timber on the rivers Tigris and Euphrates. My wish to amaze grew no less, but a healthier wish to know joined it. I sensed dimly that a great gate was opening in my world that would lead me out from the little place where I was born and had lived till now, into a whole marvellous world of learning. There was even a master called Algie Harrow, and Harrow I knew was also the name of the second-best English public school. I almost felt myself at the portals of the greatest, Eton.

Until I was ten, I was rather thin: tallish but slight. And I had inherited much of my mother's looks. For the only time in my life I could have been called nice-looking.

Then the war came: the war meant one thing to my mother. U-boats and near starvation. She often recalled 1917, when the U-boats nearly brought Britain to her knees and my mother queued all day for a piece of suet at the butcher's shop only to be turned away empty-handed as she reached the head of the queue and the suet ran out.

It became my mother's major War Effort to see that my father and I didn't starve. She would often deprive herself, saying she wasn't really hungry and would have only a piece of bread and butter. My father, who was only 8 stone and built like a whippet, and who could breathe in and display every rib in his body, simply burnt off his extra share of the food into energies for the War Effort.

I got fat. From being a slender ten-year-old in 1939, by 1941, when I reached the grammar school, I was positively elephantine. I was so fat that they weighed me and gave my mother extra clothing coupons. The first day at grammar school, as I walked in with the rest, a loud but anonymous voice called out in amazement, 'Look at that fat slug!'

The first morning in the classroom the newly appointed form captain gave the class his opinion that my father must have had amazing sexual prowess to have engendered anything as colossal as me. It was, of course, that ruthless time of pre-adolescence when one can be crucified daily for something as trivial as an overlong nose or a pair of sticking-out ears. It also meant that I was utterly and totally useless at sport. Getting changed was a twice-weekly horror. It was observed that I was so fat that I had near-female breasts, which only got another laugh from most of the form, though the ferociously oversexed and sadistic Jackie Wilson actually attempted to make sexual advances while we were lying one hot summer afternoon waiting to bat in a cricket match. Although I was not at all pugnacious at that time, enough was enough, and I managed to land him a well-placed kick that was also a comment on what I thought of his sexuality, and that at least settled that.

But if I didn't do something quickly I was certainly heading for the bottom of the peck order, and the role of form buffoon. I think I dimly realized that, boys being simple souls, everyone in the form had to be famous for something, whether the champion footballer like Jack Porterfield, or the champion farter like Kenny Russell. And you were only allowed to be famous for one thing. So if I didn't want to be famous for being fat, I'd better get famous for something else. I would be famous for being brilliant.

I worked at it like hell. My hand was always first up with the answer, and the answer was always right. To my pleasant surprise, it was as easy in the grammar school as it had been in the primary school. After the first exams I was top of the class. Being a swot was not the anathema then that it is now: equal admiration was given by boys to those who were bright and those who were good at games. And I had the wisdom to share my answers with those who wanted them. Jack Porterfield, form captain, best at football, best at fighting, was far from best at schoolwork. But he longed for academic distinction, as I longed for his footballing prowess. His hand was always up: his answers frequently so wrong he got the belly laugh from the class. There was obviously room for profitable trade between us. I picked the seat next to his, and slipped him the proper answers.

It extended outside the classroom; there, too, he was the leader of the pack. But a pack leader needs more than authority; he needs a string of bright ideas to keep the pack amused. I supplied the ideas. He was duly grateful. The next time the odious Jackie Wilson tried bullying me

Jack gave him a bloody nose. The pack found another candidate for bullying, a thin, rather effeminate boy called Walter Matthews. And later, a rather hysterical boy called Smith, who went berserk and actually foamed at the mouth if provoked enough: like being jammed halfway through a sash window three storeys up and left all lunchtime; or being hauled thirty feet up the caretaker's ash chute by putting the hook for the ash buckets through the back of his thin leather belt. All of us got caned for that, but caning in company simply promotes solidarity. I can't say I felt any contrition for either Matthews or Smith. We weren't sadistic; we simply made Matthews weep because his weeping was possible, and we made Smith foam as if he was a natural phenomenon, like the boiling mud geysers of Iceland. It staved off the boredom of wet lunch hours. The few boys who spoke up against it were disliked as insufferable prigs, Methodist ministers from the cradle, intent on crushing all the joy out of life. We simply ignored them, and made them cease to exist: we liked Matthews and Smith much better.

So I settled comfortably into my place round Jack Porterfield's throne. Until disaster struck again from the direction of my changing body. One day the teacher wrote some questions on the blackboard, and I simply couldn't see to read them. Overnight, the whole world had become a curious blur.

I don't think I was ever afraid of going blind. Perhaps because it happened so swiftly, and then got no worse. Or perhaps because I was far more afraid of something else: the spectre of being a Specky-Four-Eyes. It must be hard now to realize just how horrible this spectre was, now that men do make passes at girls who wear glasses. In those days, all the spectacles were round, with wire rims, and they made you look like an owl. They carried the coarse horror of false teeth or an artificial limb. They were snatched from your face and thrown round the class twice a day, and frequently broken. This was another means of reducing a boy to tears or to foaming at the mouth. To be a fat boy with glasses: that, I knew, was a handicap greater than even I could ever recover from.

Nobody must ever know, never, never, never: I would genuinely rather have died. And so I sat in the middle of a class, trying desperately to find the answers, trying equally desperately to find the questions.

A quick and overloud request for help to Jack Porterfield: the stupid fool couldn't make out what I wanted. The only result was a public telling-off from the teacher for trying to cheat. A second attempt brought the threat of the cane. And all around the class were busy scribbling answers which, if they were wrong, were at least relevant to the questions.

Then it occurred to me that the teacher sat just in front of the blackboard. If I got to the teacher, I got to the questions. So out I went, a thing unheard of.

'Please, sir, I can't make out that word!'

I point at random to any word. He gives me a funny look. The word is quite clearly 'and'.

'No, sir, not that word, that word'.

'The word is "Jenkin's", boy. What were the causes of the War of Jenkin's Ear?'

Allah be praised, I have question four. I have also memorized questions one to three, in the correct order. At three feet, I can read the questions quite clearly. I get back to my desk and rip off the correct answers. But that leaves questions five to seven. Inspiration is coming back.

'Please, sir, may I leave the room?'

Again I swoop in, perilously close to the teacher's desk and the blackboard.

'Well, don't stand there gawping at me, boy. Go, if you must.'

By the time I go, I have memorized questions five to seven. I run to the toilets, do a feeble pee to respect the truth, run back, and finish my answers just in time as the bell goes.

It was never to be quite so hard to deceive the class and the staff again. My marks at the end of that term were a little down; I sank to third instead of top. My report speaks of work falling off, the word 'disappointing' occurs once or twice. And the staff told my parents I had got rather 'fussy' and asked dire questions about the state of my bladder. But of course that played right into my mother's hands, and they got told all about her, and my, weak kidneys. After that, I got leave to go to the toilet whenever I felt the need. The class did not mock my kidneys: schoolboys have no interest in kidneys, which are invisible. The following term, I was back at the top again, as if nothing had happened. I had adjusted to my blurred world, and was quite happy in it: sight ceased to matter. There were no doctors to spare to give schoolboys annual medical check-ups, they were all in the forces. In a state of profound myopia I passed my School Certificate and Higher School Certificate with flying colours, played rugby, soccer and tennis, took out my first girlfriend, wept at the fall of Singapore and rejoiced at the victory of El Alamein. Thank God my reading sight was perfect, and the blackboard gave way to dictated notes as chalk became short like everything else. It remained my secret alone for six years.

Bob (extreme left) and school friends in fancy dress

Bob on his bicycle at Balkwell Green

CHAPTER EIGHTEEN

Enemies and Allies

'Japanese planes have attacked Pearl Harbor.'

I spent the whole weekend in a daze. Ridiculous that America and Japan should fight! I'd read an American comic only a month before, in which American fighters were defending San Francisco against Japanese bombers (they all had open cockpits and fixed wheels with spats, jokes by comparison with Spitfires) and I thought, how silly, how can they fight when they're on opposite sides of the world?

We started off despising the Japanese. We thought we'd beat them easily. My father would buy only British goods, or German; even in the war, he bought me German toys because they were 'well made'. Everything else was 'foreign rubbish' and worst of all was 'Japanese rubbish'. He once bought a Japanese lighter for a shilling. It worked twice, then broke. I'll never forget the gesture of disgust with which he threw it in the fire. We thought the Japanese fighter planes' wings would fall off, we thought their fleet would sink in the first storm.

Inexplicably, they didn't.

The Japs won, in the jungles of Malaya. But that was because they could climb in the trees, like the monkeys they practically were. They ran about in brainless yellow hordes, like ants. They were all exactly the same, tiny, bald, yellow, with spectacles, thin moustaches and buck teeth. They didn't need supplies like real men, they could live on beetles and nuts. And they committed atrocities, disembowelled their prisoners and staked them out for the ants to eat. They raped every female in sight, and cut steaks from the sides of living water buffalo, which then staggered about, bleeding.

And then came the Aleutian campaign, when they committed suicide in huge numbers, rather than be taken prisoner; holding a hand grenade to their bellies and then pulling out the pin.

I mean, we knew the Nazis were nasty, but in the war we were always on the lookout for the Good German: the fighter ace, shot down and entertained to dinner in the local RAF officers' mess. The compassionate U-boat commander; the shot-down bomber-gunner who was no more than a young lad, and was given a cup of tea. Nobody ever looked for a good Jap. Tolkien was writing at that time, and if you want to know how we saw the Japs then, we saw them as orcs. Or rats, or flies. If we'd had an aerosol spray that killed Japs, we'd have killed the lot.

And of course, we had. When the atomic bombs were dropped on Hiroshima and Nagasaki, we stood up in the cinema and cheered our heads off. We were deeply and vilely satisfied. Like eating a hot meat pie.

When Hitler declared war on America, I knew he was mad. Yes, I spent the whole weekend wandering in a daze, and one American song kept running through my brain.

America, I love you, you're like a mother to me . . .
From ocean to ocean, this sudden emotion . . .

And America became magic. The things we heard of!

Bulldozers that could build a whole airfield in twenty-four hours. Liberty ships built in a week, from the first plate being laid. The Americans were going to build 25,000 planes a year. There had only been 3,000 on both sides in the Battle of Britain. The war had become, as we soon learnt to say, a different ball game.

American comics flooded in. New heroes like Superman and Dick Tracy, the cop with the two-way wrist TV and nose like a rectangular kite. And jazz records we learnt to listen to the American way, heads neck-breakingly on one side, nodding wisely in time with the music, clicking our fingers to the rhythm and, if possible, chewing gum. They seemed all about travel, those records. We were urged to take the '"A" Train' or 'The Chattanooga Choochoo', especially on 'Route 66'. Americans were always arriving or departing.

We learnt that Betty Grable had the best legs in the world, and they were insured for a million dollars (the word 'million' was on every lip). Better still, she was married to Harry James, who could play 'The Flight of the Bumble Bee' on the trumpet faster than it had ever been played before.

There came a dreadful rumour (the first one not concerned with the war for two years) that she had died in childbirth.

Our other hero was Fats Waller, the huge negro who invented boogie-woogie. Every kid who got near a piano could play the left-hand roll of boogie-woogie. Fats talked to himself as he played, a shocking thing till you got used to it. We had just got used to it when he died of pneumonia. It seemed a very serious blow to the War Effort.

There were two gods of the clarinet, Benny Goodman and Artie Shaw. (I refused to believe that the American 'Artie' was only a shortening of the mundane English name 'Arthur' and I had a fight with another kid over that.) Both had their supporters, who argued interminably about their virtues, as if they were Arsenal and Tottenham Hotspur. For a while, we quite forgot about the war.

But even there, the Yanks were tops. We abandoned our faithful Hurricanes and Spitfires, which had only won the Battle of Britain. The American fighters had much more exciting names, even swearing names, like the Grumman Hellcat. Above all, there was the Flying Fortress, which carried so many guns and flew in such tight groups six miles high, that no German fighter would dare come near it. And it had a bomb-sight so accurate that it could drop a bomb into a pickle barrel from 20,000 feet.

And the American troop carriers, huge four-engined monoplanes called 'Stratocruiser' and 'Constellation' that made our old biplanes look like rubbish from the Science Museum.

I made an impassioned speech in our school debating society about the superiority of all things American. My beloved English teacher kept tripping me up, stopping me for saying things like 'Th'Americans' instead of 'The Americans'. I couldn't understand it. He'd always been sympathetic to me before.

Of course, the gilt eventually got knocked off the gingerbread. The Hellcat, for all its name, didn't do too well against the Japanese Zero. And the Americans kept on shortening their line, and making strategic withdrawals, just like we'd been doing ever since 1940. Then some Americans were stationed at Whitley Bay, and people started saying there were three things wrong with them: they were 'overpaid, oversexed and over here'. They had a fight with the Australian Air Force on the seafront, and the Australians threw several of them through the plate-glass windows of shops.

We never starved but we ate some bloody funny things. Best was American dried egg. You poured a thin trickle into the frying pan, and then as it cooked it blew up like a balloon, until it was two inches thick, like a big yellow humpback whale.

And we had whale meat, which tasted strongly of fish unless you soaked it for twenty-four hours in vinegar, after which it tasted of vinegar. But there was so much of it, great big steaks as big as your plate, that we didn't care what it tasted like.

Sausagemeat was pale pink but I don't think it had any meat in it at all. Late in the war, my mother got a pound of butcher's sausage, the sausage the butcher made for his own family. It seemed indecent, because lumps of real meat kept dropping out of it and it nearly made us sick. I lived a lot on chip butties, but you had to eat them quickly, before the chips turned dark blue.

The government posters made us all hate the 'Black Market', though no one ever knew what a 'Black Marketeer' looked like. But all through the war, things kept 'appearing' in our house. One Christmas, a whole unopened box of Mars bars. Another time a seven-pound tin of butter which for some reason we kept in the bath. I enjoyed carving great caves out of it. When I asked my father where these things came from, he'd say 'bought it off a feller at work', or 'off the ships', so matter-of-factly that it never occurred to me till after the war that my father must have 'received goods knowing them to have been stolen': from the Black Market.

Luckily we had a neighbour on the trawlers. My parents looked after his wife while he was at sea, especially when she was pregnant, so we were never short of fish. And we had the large greenhouse. Immediately after every raid my father would go and check how many panes the Germans had blown out. By the end of the war, it wasn't so much a glasshouse as a cardboard-house, but all through we had so many tomatoes we sold them to other people.

My mother felt that her patriotic duty was to fatten me up. However, our dog got very fat as well. Our neighbour in the trawlers used to see it as a good-luck mascot, and when he went on a trip, he used to come and stroke our dog first. When he came back safely, he would give our dog a whole pound block of Cadbury's chocolate. The dog used to bring it home in its mouth, with half the wrapping chewed off: my mother would immediately requisition it. The number of times we handed round tooth-marked chocolate at Christmas . . .!

We used to spend a week's holiday in Cumberland during the latter part of the war. My mother would fill her time by collecting eggs from all the surrounding farms, a dozen at a time. At first she was treated with great suspicion, as a Ministry of Ag. and Fish snooper, but, by the end of the war, she'd come home with twelve dozen in a carrier bag.

We used to stay on a farm and I'd help the farmer with the harvest. I was outraged to see POWs helping as well. No security. An army lorry with a canvas top pulled up at the farm gate, the driver banged on his door and shouted, 'Out, you idle wops', and three woebegone figures in brown leapt down from the tailgate and stood clutching bundles and shivering in the morning air.

They were known as 'Alfonso', 'Luigi' and 'That Useless Bugger', none of which were their real names. To the farmers, the first one you got was Alfonso and the second Luigi. Not knowing a word of English, they had learnt to answer to these names, like pet dogs. It helped us to distinguish them. 'You Useless Bugger' answered to his name as cheerfully as the rest.

Alfonso and Luigi were very small, about five foot four. Swarthy, hook-nosed, big-brown-eyed, they might have been twins, though they were not related. They did everything together, never more than four feet apart. The farmer had learnt not to separate them or they became miserable and their work went off. Even in the heat of midday, they kept on their greatcoats and rolled-up balaclava helmets.

The farmer said they were good workers because they came from the north of Italy and had been car workers in Turin before the war. All the ones from the north were hard workers, but those from the south were totally idle: no farmer wanted them, but they had to accept one southerner for every two northerners. Rationing!

'That Useless Bugger' (always uttered with total contempt) was from the south. Bigger, about five foot seven, slender, with a trim black moustache and arrogant air. He'd stop work the moment the farmer's eye was off him, and drift away to where the two land girls were working like, as the farmer said, 'a tomcat on heat'. Very handsome, like Douglas Fairbanks, with a flashy smile and perfect white teeth. But as far as the land girls were concerned, he didn't exist. He had learnt one English phrase: 'I can see the top of your bra!' One of the land girls turned to him, and said in broad Lancashire:

'An' I can see the top o' thy underpants an' all, and they're mucky!'

Wet lunchtimes, we sometimes shared the back of the army wagon. It was embarrassing. The English farmhands discussed the Italians as if they weren't there, really intimately, as if they were cattle. And the Italians discussed us similarly, in Italian. Had there been an interpreter, there'd certainly have been a fight.

One evening I hitched a lift back to the village in the POW truck. Getting off, over the tailgate, I caught myself awkwardly in the crotch. As I lay doubled up in agony on the road, the truck drove off to enormous Italian cheering and laughter. They seemed to think that for once they'd won a victory. It was then I realized how much they really hated us.

The German POW was different: a tall, thin, dignified figure in Africa Korps uniform that grew daily more like a farmhand's gear. He fastened up his trousers with binder-twine, just like they did. He spoke a little English, very slowly, but all the farmhands listened to him patiently. He had owned his own farm in Bavaria, before the war. All he wanted was to get back to it. He was allowed to do any job on the farm, and was allowed to go off on his own. He had shown the farmhands several agricultural tricks they didn't know and, when they were stuck, they would send for him and ask his opinion. He was very loving with animals, especially the dogs. He wouldn't leave any broken thing unmended, and spent one lunch hour mending a drystone wall that had fallen down. He was called 'Fritz', like all German prisoners, and was content to answer to it.

He worked a fiddle with the farmer, who was charged

so much an hour for his services. But however hard Fritz worked, he only got five shillings from the POW camp people. So when he'd worked eight hours, he and the farmer would sign his work-card as having worked only four. Then the farmer would give Fritz a packet of cigarettes instead. Once, when his camp-lorry broke down and didn't come for him in the evening, he walked back to the camp alone. He wished Hitler was dead, so that he could go home to his farm. He was the only one allowed inside the farmhouse, for a meal or a bath.

CHAPTER NINETEEN

Religion and Church Life

At a very early age, my mother had taught me to say my prayers. This is quite different from teaching a child to pray; you can probably only do that by praying in front of him. The first time a child sees such prayer answered, he may begin to realize that the parent is in contact with a Being of terrifying power and rather baffling temperament.

Teaching a child to say its prayers is much less ambitious: it rapidly becomes a performance to the child, something boring, slightly distasteful but essential to please mother, like kissing rather whiskery elderly aunts. I learnt my prayer easily, increasing its pace as I grew more adept, and finally got it down to a fast gabble of mumbo-jumbo, because I wanted to get on to more interesting things like reading with a torch under the bedclothes. My mother never seemed to notice: dirt left on my neck aroused much more passion. Cleanliness was obviously much more important than godliness.

The prayer itself has remained a stumbling block all my religious life. It went:

> Gentle Jesus, meek and mild,
> Look upon a little child;
> Pity my simplicity,
> Suffer me to come to Thee.

For one thing, even then I realized I had no simplicity to pity: I knew myself for a complicated, devious and cunning little creature. There was a huge man of forty living in our street who could not even write his name. His mother had to dress him in the mornings, and he could never say anything but 'Hello there! Where're you going now?' which he said over and over again. My mother told me he was 'a bit simple'. Obviously simplicity was not for me.

Then I took an instant dislike to the word 'suffer'. I have never to this day had the slightest desire to suffer, for anybody's sake. Later, I would drive myself to sculpt eight hours a day, until my eyes and legs gave out; or type until my backbone ached so much I felt only my kidneys were propping it up. I still was determined never to suffer.

But what really finished me was this meek-and-mild business. It would be another forty-five years before I read the Bible properly and discovered that Jesus, far from being meek and mild, was as argumentative as most Jews of his generation, was as verbally aggressive as a philosophy don and could be driven to physical violence to the extent of perhaps inflicting grievous bodily harm on certain moneylenders. With this meek and mild creature I wanted nothing to do. He sounded like the weak kid in the class who was always being got into a corner and beaten up half to death. One did not mix with such kids, as their unpopularity could rub off on you.

Then my mother made the even worse step of sending me to Sunday school. As neither she nor my father ever went near the church, this baffled me greatly, and one Sunday I tried the experiment of only pretending to go, and hiding myself in the outside toilet instead on the excellent grounds that if they caught me lurking there I could plead a massive and disabling attack of diarrhoea.

When boredom finally drove me back into the house on reconnaissance, they were both fast asleep under newspapers: they had bought themselves an hour's peace and quiet for the price of a penny collection money.

That penny worried me a great deal. I didn't know what to do with it. I had a sneaking feeling that Jesus mightn't be so meek and mild about being robbed of a penny. Besides, my mother would be sure to find it in my trouser pocket. I tried flushing it down the loo, when I was finally sure that the interminable hour, unmarked by any watch or clock, was up. It lay stubbornly on the bottom of the pan, under the terrifyingly infected water (my mother being certain that all germs lived down there, and that they were at least as vicious as piranha fish). I let the cistern refill, with beating heart, and flushed again in desperation. And again, and again. Finally my mother came and hammered on the door, demanding to know what sanitary end-of-the-world was in progress.

Shouting wildly about diarrhoea, I plunged my hand to the elbow into the piranha-laden water, shoved the penny in my pocket, and emerged. I spent the evening knowing I would certainly and rapidly die from a raging disease that spread across my whole body from my elbow and the still-damp patch on my leg from my pocket. And then I would face my wrathful maker who would want to know about that penny. Perhaps that sin was the one that destroyed Sodom and Gomorrah, or drowned the world in Noah's time.

But the next day it was the penny that got buried, not me. After that, I went regularly to Sunday school; it was simply less bother. But it offended me greatly. It was not a proper school. Proper schools had pretty young women who sold interesting ideas in bright lively voices. Proper schools had toys, and let you draw triremes and centurions. The Sunday-school teachers were bent old ladies in flowered hats, who wouldn't answer my questions. And then, one day, I realized that they couldn't answer my questions. I found my lifelong greatest joy, the asking of awkward questions. If God was three, how could He be One? I turned it into a maths sum, on the tiny blackboard. If Jesus was the Son of God, how could he be the son of David? Was David God's grandfather? I raised hell. I reduced the elderly ladies in the flowered hats to tears. No hooliganism; no vandalism; no rudeness. Nothing that could be punished (I had realized that they didn't have the cane in Sunday school) or worse, reported to my mother. I was passed from class to class like a parcel.

I remember the vicar had finally to take me on one side threatening that if I didn't stop it, that he would 'drop on me like a ton of bricks'. This gave me pause; not that I was scared, more awed. The phrase was new to me, and I loved new phrases: I was also uncertain whether or not he could actually turn himself into bricks. He wore a long black skirt instead of trousers and cycle-clips and, for all I knew, he might wear black knickers under his long black skirt. He also wore a massive scarred brown leather belt, with a large gold cross hanging off it. He wasn't married and had no children, though everyone called him Father Pestle. He also looked at me, not with rage or annoyance, but with a terrible sadness, and that was much more terrifying, as if he knew about the buried penny and my impending terrible disease. He was also, possibly, a really holy man, and all my life I have avoided really holy men. In short, he was as totally alien as a creature from Mars, and one didn't muck about with aliens of unknown powers. I capitulated. Just turned off altogether, and sat like a wooden duck in Sunday school, thinking of higher things like the mystery of the *Marie Celeste*, or if werewolves really existed.

About this time, there was a sort of explosion in church life. Not only a new church, but a new vicar, the Revd Forbes T. Horan. An exotic species to have swum into our parts, an Oxford or Cambridge running Blue who had even married the bishop's daughter. All the ladies were convinced that he would go far; they were convinced that we had a future Archbishop of Canterbury. He was good-looking too, in a long-limbed aristocratic sort of way. I don't know which of these things caught my mother's imagination (I suspect it was marrying the bishop's daughter) but she began going to church and, out of pure curiosity, I went with her. I was convinced by this time that most things adults did were far more interesting than most things children did.

There were two immediate pluses. The new church had an open timber roof of the most complicated design and, when boredom got too much, I would lift my eyes with apparent piety to Heaven, and imagine I was a small but agile mouse pioneering new routes along the complex beams from one part of the church roof to another. Many was the pious lady who, after church, praised my holiness and wondered aloud what godly thoughts must have been passing through my mind on these occasions.

The other was the language of the service. It was like learning a foreign language, but a surprisingly easy one, and quite enough to baffle my stupid contemporaries. And it gave rise to some marvellous images if taken literally.

'Almighty God, unto whom all hearts are open, all desires known, and from whom no secrets are hid . . .' Cranmer, who wrote it, may have meant it to strike terror into my heart, instead he struck wonder. I had visions of throbbing pink hearts with little doors opening into them and, much better, a God who was a kind of super Sherlock Holmes, complete with deerstalker hat and bloodhound. Being an intensely nosy little boy, I warmed to this God. Perhaps, when I eventually went to Heaven, all the secrets would be revealed to me too. This was a God whose 'Property was always to have mercy'. In other words, he was a colossal landlord, (this was confirmed by 'In my Father's house are many mansions'). I very much wanted to explore those mansions, especially if they were all as interesting as this church roof. The hymns, too, were never-ending fountains of crazy surrealist imagery. Hymn 220 in 'Ancient and Modern' particularly:

'Till moons shall wax and wane no more' gave me a moon made entirely of white candlewax.

'And infant voices shall proclaim their early blessings on His Name' gave me a mass of babies all in their prams suddenly bursting out singing. Then there were prisoners leaping to 'loose their chains', like a mass of penal acrobats. I was rather more dubious about 'the weary finding eternal rest' which sounded pleasantly sinister, and I wondered who the mysterious 'Sons of Want' were, and why they should be blessed in particular. They sounded to me a bit like Indian thugs, who made their hard-up-ness an excuse to do unmentionable things. Jesus' 'name like incense shall arise': fancy, a name materializing like a genie, then turning to smoke and, presumably after arising, it would vanish, genie-like, back into its bottle. Such fancies as these helped me over the more boring parts of the service, which remain in my mind as a complete blank. As a grammar-school boy I took particular pleasure in a verse of Newman's 'Praise to the holiest in the height', where it goes:

O generous love! that He, who smote
In Man for man the foe,
The double agony in Man
For man should undergo.

I liked this because it was difficult to understand and yet had a very tight use of language: just like a theorem in geometry at school. Once I had understood it, I used to take it out and polish it frequently, as a living proof that you had to be bright to be a Christian: it was no religion for 'thickies', and B-streamers need not apply. Under the care of Forbes T. Horan (who after all had been to Oxford or Cambridge) I was nourishing an intellectual pride worthy of total damnation.

In other ways Forbes was a sad disappointment. He organized a church sports day with exotic races like the '220 yards' or the '440 yards' which sounded very dashing compared with my primary school's sack race or three-legged race. We all turned up to see our sprinting vicar whack the pants off the men of the congregation. The men were deeply looking forward to it too as they all liked to see a thing brilliantly done. But Forbes was strangely reluctant to take part. When finally prevailed upon, by universal demand, he took off his blazer for the 220, his best distance. The pistol cracked. Perhaps that made him forget himself. He went off like a rocket and was instantly ten yards ahead. Then he unaccountably slowed down and came in nearly last, quite unpuffed, hardly breathing heavily. We were all, including the men in the congregation, deeply disappointed. My mother said he had lost the race through Christian humility: it made me deeply suspicious of Christian humility for the rest of my life.

Then there was one evening, after the service, when my mother stayed behind to talk to Forbes in some distress. She could not persuade my father to come to church. Forbes, a little agitated, swept round and round the church aisles at some speed, his long legs swishing his cassock, my mother trying very hard to keep up with him, and me desperately trotting behind. Forbes urged on my mother patience and prayer: God would bring him in the end. I found this all very alarming. Could prayer actually change things? I mean, besides pleasing my mother and getting me an extra biscuit? Were Forbes and my mother and God in a plot against my father? Should I warn my father of this Goddish plot? After all, three against one didn't seem very fair. But I had endless faith in my father: I was sure that he could cope even with God.

But God (or Forbes) proved too cunning. They got my father in the only possible way he could be got. Forbes turned up at our house, looking distressed. The church garden was in a terrible state: would my father help him out with it? I think my father would have helped the Devil or even Hitler himself with his garden, if the garden had been a mess and the Devil or Hitler had asked nicely. One evening my father departed with his spade. Three hours later he returned to water his own. But his gait was unsteady, and he couldn't seem to direct the watering can at the particular plant he had in mind. Also, he kept laughing to himself.

It came out that after the hot work, Forbes had invited

all the men back to the vicarage for refreshment, and had offered my father a glass of something brown and fizzy. So, at the hands of Mother Church, as my father always said afterwards, he let alcohol in the form of a shandy pass his lips for the first time in his life. The shadow of Granda's drinking had been lifted from him, and he was as drunk as a lord on a half-pint of shandy.

It shook my mother to the core, but by that time we were definitely a church family. Who was this God who worked by drink and deceit? A God who plotted in the dark and could summon the demon drink, I wondered darkly.

Some of the sermons increased my suspicions. There was the missionary, who told me as I crouched as low as possible in my seat that God wanted me to go out to Africa immediately and nurse lepers. Lepers were people who had no noses, no fingers and thumbs, and this made me very reluctant. But if I let God into my life (here the missionary fixed me with burning eyes) he would sweep me there instantly. I felt like a limpet, desperately clinging to home and school, while God became an enormous wave who, given an inch, would sweep me away and before I could blink I should be spooning gruel into a lipless black mouth.

I clung on all the harder.

Then there was the sermon about the Boy Who Gave Things Up. He trained himself to give up the orange he dearly wanted to a friend. There was no possibility of sharing the orange: the friend had no particular desire or need for the orange. The little saint was simply training himself to Give Things Up For God. I thought we had a right nutter here, who would certainly come to a sticky end. I was right: the little saint went on to give up his pocket money to church missions, and his holiday to a little crippled boy. With such madness the end could not be far off; confinement to the large walled house up the road, the mention of whose name always raised an uneasy laugh among the adults? No, he went on a voyage, and of course the ship sank, and the nutter gave up his place in the lifeboat to somebody who needed it more, and he happily and blessedly drowned. Because he had trained himself to Give Things Up. I felt like rushing for the exit there and then, as if the church had become a burning cinema.

But worst of all was the visiting preacher who preached about Hell Fire. The church was especially full on this occasion: everyone was looking forward to it. The preacher was a rather fat man, and bald. Everyone said he would, as he reached his heights of oratory, thump his fists in rage on the pulpit. I wanted to see that bit. So he told us what happened to sinners after they died: up to their eyes in burning brimstone. If you want to know what it will feel like, hold your hand in a candle flame for a second when you get home tonight. And that will be for just one second: Hell is for all eternity.

I'd never known the congregation leave the church so happy and animated. I suppose he was the forerunner of the horror movie, the video nasty, and he had really given them their money's worth. They were delighted. As one old lady said to another with satisfaction, 'There's nothing I like better than a good hellfire sermon. What are you giving Jim for supper tonight?'

I was deeply disappointed. He sounded to me like the tired old ham actor who was once asked by school to give us 'Great Scenes from Shakespeare'. His fists were soft and pudgy, and when he hammered on the pulpit, he took good care not to hurt them. I felt he wasn't thinking about God at all, he was just giving his audience what they expected.

But still, in a world without television, a world with radios famous chiefly for their fading batteries and crackling atmospherics, a world where the cinema cost good money, the Church was the main way of satisfying my growing taste for peculiar things.

I sometimes wondered whether to go into the Church in a big way, to join the business and throw in my lot with them. I wondered how successful the Church was, and whether it could help me to 'get on in life', like the Freemasons. Was God a good employer? (I even once considered whether I should join the Nazi Party, if the Germans managed to conquer England, in 1940. They had rather impressive uniforms, and would hardly shoot their own members. Perhaps the Nazi Party helped you to get on?)

Really, joining the Church meant joining the choir, and walking into church in a long file, wearing grand-looking black-and-white vestments and looking incredibly holy, like some of my friends. It also meant getting confirmed, having the bishop lay his hands on you or, in the parlance of my mother and her friends, getting 'done'. All the girls seemed to be getting 'done': it became a fashion, like getting engaged. They all yakked and yakked about what dresses they would wear, and having a veil on their heads, and sitting in the front of the church where, miraculously, a ray of sunlight always seemed to come through the window and smite them at the appropriate moment. After being done with sunlight, my mother asked me whether I would like to be 'done' properly.

It seemed a chance to get into the public eye so I said OK.

This then meant attending confirmation classes at the vicarage. Forbes T. Horan having by this time departed for another parish, the new vicar was a very busy man. He was also always late for the classes. We would be shown by his slight demure wife into his study which was overpoweringly holy with huge, dark, uncomfortable chairs, a massive desk with all kinds of unknown and doubtless holy objects on it, and above his chair and behind the desk a large, dark and agonized crucifix. The crucifix appalled me. It was all very well in church, at a range of 50 feet, but here it was staring at me not 5 feet away. It overpowered the room, like a huge cold draught from another world, or the smell of disinfectant in hospitals. God was listening; God was watching; He filled the room; He penetrated into my soul, where the penny still lurked.

Unfortunately, it did not seem to penetrate the head of one Ginger Stevenson at all. He was a third year at the grammar school, where we were all first years. And he had to show off in front of us kids. So, with an ear warily cocked for the sound of the vicar's bicycle, he got behind the desk, sat in the vicar's chair, clasped his hands together in the vicar's holy steeple, and hummed and hawed in the vicar's voice, saying that the first confirmation class was about how babies were made. He then went into a full and lucid description leaving no detail out.

This account tallied fairly reasonably with the dirty song I had rejected two years previously as being anatomically impossible. I realized with a sinking feeling that it must be accurate. But what was much worse, I looked at the crucifix over his head. God was watching; God was listening.

I edged my chair back a little so that when the thunderbolt from above hit Stevenson in the midst of his blasphemy, I would stand no chance of being caught by the fallout.

But no thunderbolt came. Stevenson babbled on unscathed; God's attention must be elsewhere. Stevenson asked, vicar-like, whether we had any questions at this point, any difficulties. Still in an abstracted daze, I awaited the thunderbolt, and wondered how Stevenson would look after it hit him. Just asleep, or dead and stiff like one of my unfortunate rabbits, or really charred to a cinder, like something out of a horror movie?

But now Stevenson, duly pleased by our gaping mouths and horrified faces, was excelling himself, passing on his version of the sex life of the vicar and his wife in a blow-by-blow account. By this time I was not so much expecting the thunderbolt as actively praying for it.

But all that arrived was the vicar on his noisy bicycle. The blasphemer had whipped round the table and put on his best holy choirboy expression before the vicar opened his study door. Then the vicar sat down, cocked up one leg to reveal perfectly ordinary trousers, and took off his cycle-clips.

At that point I lost my faith for the first time. If God could not look after his own, He either had no guts or no thunderbolts, or else He didn't exist.

I was confirmed by the Bishop of Newcastle some weeks later in a state of perfect and complete atheism. The regulation miraculous ray of sunlight smote me like all the rest. The bishop seemed to sense something was up: he seemed to keep his hands on my head longer than anybody else's. He seemed to be trying with all his might and main to force some kind of power through my skull, but I could feel it not getting through, and bouncing off again.

Still, my mother was pleased I'd been 'done', like all the rest.

CHAPTER TWENTY

Rugby

I had my troubles at Tynemouth High School. I progressed with painful slowness from the fat boy who was hopeless at games to the ferociously muscled monster of the First Rugby XV, but I always felt at home, a fish deeply in water.

My weight problem solved itself. Around 1944, the mass of blubber began inexorably to turn into a mass of muscle. I found, building a rockery for our scout hut, that I could lift rocks that beat the famous Jack Porterfield. On scout hikes, he was amazed to find that though he could still run faster than me, I could walk him off his legs. In the changing room one of the class mocked my still-melting flab and I simply, in my rage, picked him up by the blazer-shoulders and held him up there, kicking and dangling, for all of five minutes. Everyone was oddly impressed when I put him down, and I was never mocked again. By the time I was fifteen I was six feet tall, and twelve and a half stone with very broad shoulders and a forty-inch chest.

And then, after long sad years failing to be any good at soccer whatever, of dancing in helpless rage while a quicker opponent tapped the ball from foot to foot under my nose, I discovered rugby. In rugby you didn't have to be quick, just big and strong and long-winded and tough. You could grab hold of gadfly-quick opponents and flatten them. You could grab the ball and head for the line carrying four opponents on your back and another one clinging to each ankle. Even being knocked flat in the mud was oddly exhilarating. There came the incredible day that, playing against Tynemouth School at Prior's Park, I not only frightened the opposing scrum-half into a jelly by throwing him into touch with the ball still in his hands, but I also scored three tries in quick succession and led their massacre to the tune of 35–0. The glory of hearing my name on every spectator's lips, hearing watching staff say, 'His name is Westall', of hearing the screeches of 'Go on, Westall, go on!' as they had long since called 'Go on, Porterfield, go on!' I was a household name. In my new-found arrogance, I got on the house team at tennis, neatly judging the foot-wide fuzzy white cloud that was the ball on to the foot-wide fuzzy brown blur that was my racquet-head. I read about the First World War fighter ace, Mickey Mannock, who only got into the RFC by learning the eye-test sight card by heart before his medical and then shot down seventy-four assorted red, blue and yellow blurs that were German fighters. Mickey Mannock and I could do anything.

It couldn't last. The war ended, the doctors came home and, one morning just before leaving school, I was caught in a snap-check with a sight-reading card by a fuzzily pretty lady doctor who had just admired my enormous chest development. I gave in without a qualm. I had taken out girls and kissed them in the back row of the pictures; I had played in the all-age county team with the famous Fenwick Allison, who was to go on and play for England. I was going on to university where more than half the profs wore spectacles, and no one called them 'Specky-Four-Eyes': spectacles were a sign of intellect.

'Have you noticed bother with your eyes recently?' asked the pretty doctor.

'Not really,' I said, quite truthfully.

The optician was a Masonic friend of my father's: he wouldn't let me suffer round owl-like wire-rims; he sold us intellectual Woodrow Wilson rimless at cost price. When he put them on me the first thing I noticed with the new-found clarity was that his kindly face was a mass of blackheads. I enjoyed the new-found clarity, reading the church clock's time from half a mile away. And yet I saw clearly quite a lot of things I didn't like about the world: it was the end of a sort of innocence. The maddening thing was that I thought the spectacles would improve my tennis no end, but I still hit the white ball with no more accuracy than I'd hit the large white blur.

I'd like to think my loss of fat was my mother relaxing after the defeat of the U-boats, but even when I was training for the final county rugby trial of 1948, by then a walloping hulk of twelve and a half stone, she would go on at me because I was too thin, and if I starved myself any more I would make myself ill. Meanwhile, my father continued to display every rib of his eight-stone body without arousing the least anxiety in her.

At Tynemouth High there was never again any teacher a hundredth part as mad or bad as Mr Barnett. Some were a little grumpy; some were real sweeties, but only three men stand out. Only three men shaped and hewed me, and I still carry the mark of their chisels.

Major Joseph Smedley, wartime headmaster, a suitably Churchillian figure with his gown and coat open and his thumbs tucked, Churchill-like, into his waistcoat pockets.

We assumed he smoked huge cigars, but of course only in private. He caned occasionally, but only for unmentionable thuggery in the toilets, which we all thoroughly approved of. His aim was to make us gentlemen, English gentlemen. He frequently addressed us as 'Gentlemen!' When, in the upper sixth, I grew a massive moustache that for some reason drove the unlikeable head of biology into public tantrums, Joe had me in for a quiet chat in his study, and asked me to shave it off as a personal favour and for the honour of the school. The appeal worked, and I got my reward in my leaving testimonial, in which he called me 'of gentlemanly bearing and manners'.

The best thing about Joe was that sometimes in assembly he would unbutton and talk to us as equals, about some aspect of the war, such as a tragic bombing or a small British victory. He warned us not to expect too much of life, and not to count our chickens before they hatched.

'On the 17th September 1917, my commanding officer on the Western Front said to me, "Smedley, I'm putting you up for the Military Cross." The next day came the great German offensive, and by noon the commanding officer was dead and I was a prisoner of war.'

After I left, we corresponded occasionally until he died at the early age of sixty-three. In his last letter he wrote, 'Pray for me that I might recover sufficiently to die at my desk in harness.' Sadly, he never did. But if there is anything left of an honourable English gent in me, Joe Smedley put it there. If there is a sense of decency in my books, I owe it to him.

Stan Liddell, head of English, captain of the Tynemouth Home Guard, hero of my novel *The Machine-Gunners*. If Joe showed me decency, Stan showed me brilliance. Classical

English good looks, the dead-straight nose, the strong jaw that would clamp decisively round a dirty old short pipe, and a moustache like Lord Kitchener's. He also had that raffish dowdiness that was the mark of his class. His was the first sports coat I saw with leather elbow-patches and leather binding round the cuffs. (When we were allowed sports coats instead of school uniform in the sixth form, my mother had to sew cuffs and patches on a brand-new coat.) While teaching, he would hitch up his faded pullover and stick his thumbs through his braces. He rode to school on the most oily and decrepit old black bicycle that you could imagine, that had a basket on the handlebars and was clearly a relic from his Cambridge days. For he was a Cambridge man, and rumour had it that he had ruined a brilliant career 'over some woman' which made him an even more romantic figure in our eyes. He has left his mark on my dress: I have followed his dowdiness while never coming within a mile of matching his elegance. I simply look a shambles. And I judge people by their dress, the opposite way from which most people do. The more sartorially a shambles a man is, the more I take to him. If a man has to wrap himself in a three-hundred pound suit, an expensive overcoat and a Jaguar car before he can show his face to the world, then he has some weakness he is hiding. Or so says the voice of my prejudice.

Stan had an intellectual arrogance that made him tremendously exciting. He would make some controversial statement, then challenge the brightest in the class to prove him wrong (having told us there was some flaw in his argument, if only we had the wit to find it). We would spend whole periods hurling ourselves at him, like a pack of hounds on some magnificent stag. He had no mercy; if we said something silly, he would send us flying, to the laughter of the rest of the class. We never really caught him out, but he taught me that getting on your feet and debating was the most exciting game in the world, and the hours flew by. He made me into a public speaker without fear, and has given me a taste for arguing about anything that has lasted all my life. One day, he said to us that he knew the inner meaning of Coleridge's poem, *The Rime of the Ancient Mariner*, and asked us to guess it. We failed. The bell rang and he gathered up his books and swept out before he could tell us. We forgot to ask him next lesson, and we never did find out that inner meaning. But, sometimes, when I lie awake before sleep, forty years later, I still try to work out what he must have meant. That's some mark he left on me.

He was the first person who told me I could become a real writer, if only I could stay 'honest' long enough. I was thirty years working out what he meant by honesty.

Puggie Anderson was as humble a teacher as Stan Liddell was arrogant. He had crept, in late middle age, from the torment of a slum caning secondary school into the academic peace of the High School, and he had the half-crushed and grateful look of one who knows he has survived with his sanity intact by the skin of his teeth. He was given all the odds and bobs of lessons that other better qualified teachers didn't want. He was a filler-up of the chinks in the timetable, of which any competent high school needs a couple. He was such a filler-in that we never worked out what he had taken his degree in. But he took sports lessons and library invigilation, and the first years in almost any subject from physics to religious knowledge. And he took our sixth form for their discussion group in the last lesson on a Friday afternoon.

Puggie's strength in this discussion period was that he never said anything. He just sat with his head on his hand and listened to us in silence, smiling gently, as we ranted on in our noisy undisciplined way.

And then we noticed something. Sometimes he would give a little tiny nod. What could this little tiny nod mean? Did it mean he agreed with us? But he gave little tiny nods for Socialist points and little tiny nods for Tory points, and even the occasional tiny nod for a Communist point. (A good third of us were Communists at seventeen. When you are seventeen, being a Communist made you feel strong and brave and forward-looking and uncompromising: it also had the delicious effect of sending your parents into gratifying hysterics.)

Anyway, it slowly dawned on us that the nod meant that we had made a valid and logical point. Puggie wasn't into politics: he was into logic and reason. In the same way, if we made a bad illogical point, a look of disgust would drift across his face, as if he had suddenly swallowed a lemon. He would close his eyes and shake his head with an infinitely weary sadness that bore some resemblance to the look on the face of the figure on our church crucifix. We gathered that unreason and illogic caused Puggie actual physical pain.

And so, with him, we learnt not just to shout our mutually contradictory prejudices at each other, but to actually confer together (if explosively) and come to voted conclusions. The most controversial motion we ever passed, in the victorious year of 1945, was that because of the bombing of Dresden and Hiroshima, Churchill and Truman should be put on trial as war criminals, alongside the Nazis at Nuremberg. I think that at this point Puggie became a little alarmed at the logical Frankenstein's monster he had let loose on the world, but by then it was too late. One of our lot, Dennis Coe, actually became a Labour MP; the rest of us have carried on our anarchistic subversion elsewhere, mainly in pubs I would guess.

Bob with his parents

Bob with Nana

PART THREE

1948–1957 Further Education

Durham University, King's College, First-class (Honours) Degree
BA in Fine Art 1953

National Service 1953–1955
Royal Corps of Signals

University of London, Slade School
Postgraduate Degree in Fine Art 1957

COMMENT

In the autumn of 1948 Bob Westall went up to King's College, Durham University, to read for an Honours Degree in Fine Art. At that time King's College was conveniently situated in Newcastle-upon-Tyne, not far from his home in North Shields. After a five-year course he gained a First Class Honours degree, majoring in sculpture. Henry Moore, the famous sculptor, came to judge the work in a final exhibition. Bob met him, talked to him, and answered the questions that Moore put to him about his work. To his amazement Moore offered him a two-year scholarship on the spot. However, from 1947 until 1963 a two-year period of compulsory conscription called National Service operated for young men. Bob Westall was twenty-four years old when in 1953 he became a Lance Corporal in the Royal Corps of Signals. He saw service in Egypt. Two years later, in 1955, he became a postgraduate scholarship student at the Slade School, London University. Writing was the least of his ambitions, with two exceptions.

Lindy McKinnel

CHAPTER TWENTY-ONE

Early Writing

I think I was a bad writer, the worst kind of writer, from the time I could first hold a pencil. I wrote my first novel in the summer holidays when I was twelve. I wrote it because I had lost all my friends from Chirton School. When I went to Tynemouth High School, they went off to the slum secondary modern, God help them. And the trouble with all my lovely new High School friends was that they lived about five miles away, in much posher houses than ours, and I was desperately shy. So, in the boredom of the long holiday, I wrote *The Mystery of Dead Man's Bay*. It was execrable. The police inspector got his first clue when the crooks dropped a crate of heroin on his foot. But it was twelve thousand words long, and that showed early stamina, if nothing else. In the loneliness of the four summer holidays that followed, I wrote four novels of increasing length and increasingly comprised of hopeless clichés borrowed from bad war movies and my parents' cowboy novels. I wrote a novel about the Pacific War, but I couldn't bear to let the Japanese have the slightest victory and, in my novel, the Japanese War ended with the destruction of the entire Japanese army, navy and air force on Wake Island in 1942. Then the hero (the son of the victorious American commander) walked off, happy ever after, into the sunset, presumably over a Mount Everest of Japanese corpses. In other words I had been entrapped by the two classical snares of the teenage novelist: total self-indulgent wish-fulfilment and the reuse of a mass of clichés already third-hand and third-rate. I never dreamt of writing about my own life and times as I regarded these as being so insufferably dull and boring that no one would want to read of them. Nevertheless, my last teenage novel was forty-five thousand words of well-spelt and punctuated prose, logically arranged in chapters and paragraphs. The matter was rubbish, but the manner was already there.

Then I discovered Tynemouth tennis courts. I invested in a second-hand tennis racquet and, with my bicycle, suddenly had a whole new social life. I didn't go to the homes of my posh friends and, therefore, had no reason to invite them back to mine. At our tennis-court social club we met, played, ate ice creams and drank soft drinks and did some early courting, winter and summer. As my social life increased, my life as a writer vanished to the point where even handing in my school essays became a painful chore. With a couple of exceptions I stayed dead as a writer for the next few years.

The first exception sprang from my need, as ever, to amaze. In the summer holiday of 1948 our entire sixth form were invited to help turn a derelict stately home, fifty miles away, into a new conference centre. We were all supposed to travel together by bus, but I had a new girlfriend in the party whom I wanted to impress, and I knew I couldn't do that by travelling with her in a bus full of yakking kids.

So I decided to ride there solo on my decrepit bicycle. Of course, the place happened to be Otterburn, a hard uphill ride across wild and desolate moors. I spent one of the few sleepless nights of my life, pondering on the terrors of disgrace. I hadn't ridden a distance anything like fifty miles and it was steeply uphill all the way to the Scottish border at Carter Bar. Suppose my bike gave out? Suppose my legs gave out? I had visions of being passed by the bus full of jeering kids, stuck at a crossroads with a collapsed wheel. Or plodding on foot across a moor, under the very eyes of my new and beautiful inamorata.

It was not to be borne. I got up at half past five and joined my father at breakfast as he got ready for the morning shift. We left the house together at ten to six. And for the first twenty miles I rode like a dervish, head down, sweating, hair flogging in my eyes, seeing nothing. Then I looked at my watch. It was only seven, my bike had held together so far, my legs were hardly even aching and I knew I was going to make it.

The whole world changed, as if a wizard had waved his wand: I realized it was the most beautiful morning, cool and sunlit. And I had the empty road all to myself: everybody was still asleep. I rode on more slowly, taking in every detail: the wide fields of cut corn, with the stooks sending long shadows across the stubble; the pair of carthorses looking over a gate, who neighed at me and blew long dragon-like streams of steam from their nostrils into the cool air. The hiss of my tyres on the dew-jewelled road, the cobwebs hung with droplets in the sunlit hedges; the blackened colliers returning home on their equally black bicycles, who nodded how-do as if I was an equal. The whole world was mine because there was no one else who wanted it at that particular moment. A layer of dull grey skin seemed to have been peeled off my eyes for the first time, and I marvelled at everything as if under a microscope. All seemed to pass slowly enough for me to enjoy it at leisure.

I had visualized arriving in Otterburn amidst cheers, in time for lunch. I arrived before nine and was offered breakfast. Everybody, staff as well as students, was deeply impressed. The week, and my relationship with Doreen, got off to a flying start.

Within a month I was in educational hell again. I had started at Newcastle to read Fine Art. From being a pretty big fish in a very small pond of five hundred kids, I was a minnow in a university of three and a half thousand, all of whom knew exactly where they were going and what they were doing, except me. It felt like a huge education factory in which for three days I was kept queuing, being interviewed, being addressed in endless streams of jargon by total strangers I never saw again, and pressure-sold things I didn't want, like joining the Officers' Training Corps. In the Art School, they had no time for my fancy artistic ideas: day after day I drew the outlines of bottles and, worse, the shapes between the bottles. Three professors prowled round behind our bent backs, sighing and tutting at our incompetence, and making very rude remarks to each other. From wanting to impress, I was battling to survive. People were thrown out without warning, if one line was put wrong. No one bothered to explain the purpose of what we were doing; we were supposed to work it out for ourselves. I just kept my head down dully and went home every night in a black rage, and in terror of letting down my parents who could no longer help me in this new hell, but who implicitly trusted me to be my usual genius.

One particular night I got to the bus station in the darkness and pouring rain, and looked up to see a bus pass with the glowing sign 'Otterburn'. A wave of bitterness flooded over me like I had never known. How could the world be so treacherous, so wonderful one minute and so dreadful the next? And then I decided I would show up this treacherous world for what it was, as a warning to other poor souls like me. I went home and wrote non-stop for three hours, calling my article 'Three Roads to Otterburn'. And in my rage and pain, I captured both the wonder of that particular morning and the horror of that particular evening. It was only published in the Old Students Section of our school magazine *The Nor' Easter* but when I next saw Stan Liddell he said, 'You'll make a writer, if you go on writing honestly about what you know.'

In 1955 I became a postgrad student at the Slade School, carving funny shapes. Stone and plaster were my whole delight until an evening in 1956. Russia had invaded Hungary, Israel was invading Egypt, the British had landed in the Suez Canal zone, and Russia was threatening to go to war with us over it. All that day I'd been patting at my clay model in a feeble and pointless way, while we all discussed the coming war. One lad had registered with some recruiting agency to go and fight in Hungary against the Russians; our gentle Jew had signed up to go and fight for Israel. I, fresh out of doing my National Service with the British Army, was expecting any moment to be called back. I kept on trying to remember bits of my training. 'Actions to take if a machine gun jams', and 'The infantry platoon in attack.' I could remember nothing coherently; I knew that if the war came I wouldn't last five minutes.

I rode home by bus in the dark and rain. I got off at Westminster Abbey. A street light was shining through the high iron railings on to the lawns within. The lawns were covered with tiny white crosses that shimmered in a ghostly way in the lamplight, all the way up to the abbey itself. It was about the time of Remembrance Sunday, and the dead of two world wars had come back to join, or warn, us. I leaned against the railings and thought dully, 'Oh, God, does it have to happen again?'

Then a voice spoke up behind me, and I turned to see a bearded Portuguese sculptor that I worked with. He said, 'We're doing a peaceful torchlight procession past the Russian Embassy, to protest about Hungary. Come and join us.'

There were ten thousand students in that procession, and we passed through the West End in an endless silent column. I remember looking up and seeing a wealthy woman standing out on her first-floor balcony, holding up her small son so he could watch. I suddenly had a vision of us all, as seen through the youngster's eyes, the wet shining street, the long dark silent column, the flickering torches, and I thought, 'For him we will be part of history; he will tell his grandchildren about seeing us when he is a very old man.'

The procession processed peacefully, and we heard a moving and liberal speech. Then the well-meaning liberal organizer asked us, through a loudspeaker mounted on a van, to complete our dignified protest by dispersing peaceably. I thought at the time he seemed rather nervous. I remember wondering why. Then somebody shouted, 'To the Russian Embassy!' and in a minute ten thousand people were running blindly, a mob. I suppose we got there because the first person to run knew the way back; nobody else did. Our mood was utterly changed, by a solitary shout. But what was our new mood? Partly, like children, we didn't want the party to end: we wanted more fun. Secondly, we enjoyed being ten thousand strong and didn't want to break up. But, mainly, we wanted to make some Russians very afraid, as they had made the Hungarians very afraid. I don't think we meant any real harm or damage, but we had this picture of the Russian ambassador cowering behind closed shutters with his staff, white-faced and mumbling prayers, as the sound of our roars echoed.

In any case, the police were there before us, a solid band four-deep across the end of the road. This baffled us immensely. How did they know we were going to attack the Russian Embassy? We hadn't known ourselves ten minutes ago! I stared at the silent disciplined ranks of coppers with mixed feelings. They had three burly superintendents in front of them, grand in a mass of silver rank badges and carrying long swagger sticks. Until now, policemen had been my friends; they told you the time, or how to get to places, or showed you across the road when you were small. And though they looked disciplined and silent and impressive, there weren't very many of them. Two hundred to our ten thousand. I felt sorry for them: they were only doing their job.

Then somebody raised a Hungarian flag, and that did it. We hurled ourselves upon the policemen with about as much fury as a crowd elbowing to get aboard a tube train in the rush hour. I swear some of us said, 'Excuse me, officer', and apologized for standing on their feet. In the end, it was a kind of rugby scrum of civilized pushing. In between, we rested and talked to the police in a mutually shy way. We asked them if they were getting paid overtime; they replied that they'd much rather be at home watching the telly. We offered them cigarettes and sweets. It was a very British occasion.

But we did break their ranks twice; twice we got six blokes into the embassy garden, over the high wall. There, being decent English guys, they hadn't a clue what they wanted to do. They stood and waved to us, and we cheered them wildly. Then the police came and arrested them, and they went away quietly, to more cheers. It might have ended in this good-humoured way if the superintendents hadn't put the mounted police in to break us up. Perhaps they were tired of paying their constables overtime, perhaps there was something they wanted to watch on the telly.

Mounted police always change the mood. Mounted police are thoroughgoing hateworthy bastards. They push the sides of their horses into your face. They rear their horses' hooves above your head. From humour, we changed in a second to blind fury. A police horse stood on my foot: all ten hundredweight of it. I punched its belly in agony and fury. A huge superintendent, with a face puce with rage said, 'Touch that horse again, lad, and I'll put you inside.'

I screamed back, 'When the revolution comes I'll see you're the first to go.' And I meant it; I'd have hanged him from the nearest lamp-post at that point. If I'd had a gun I would have shot him. That's what police horses do to you. It seems ironic, in retrospect, that while I was threatening the Red Revolution, I was actually attacking the Russian Embassy.

Anyway, in the end they broke us up, but not until a police horse had shoved its backside through the window of an expensive dress shop and its rider emerged draped in the latest Paris fashion. The horses harried us all the way to the tube station, and we had to fight to the end to protect the girls from harm.

I got home after midnight. My flat was silent but I was

much too worked up to sleep. I imagined all the newspapers printing the story, the police and government version of the story, blackening the names of the naughty students and making us seem like silly children who had misbehaved at a party. Why should they have a monopoly of the news? I sat down and wrote, until four in the morning, exactly how it had been for us. Four thousand words longhand. Then I walked out into the dawn and posted it to my home newspaper the *Newcastle Journal*.

A week later my mother wrote to ask when I was being sent to prison, but you could tell that she was pleased really. The *Newcastle Journal* had printed the whole thing. Three weeks later they sent me a cheque for three guineas without a word. That was the first bit of professional writing I ever had published. I wasn't to publish again for five years: it was just that once again, a moment, a happening, a mood, had grabbed the writer in me by the scruff of the neck.

PART FOUR

*1958–1993 Marriage, Christopher
and 'The Machine-Gunners'*

CHAPTER TWENTY-TWO

'The Machine-Gunners' and Marni

My life moved on; I finished my postgrad degree, took up teaching art in a tough inner-city school in Birmingham, got married, and then I got a better job in Yorkshire. In 1960 my son was born, and I moved to Cheshire as head of art in a four-hundred-year-old grammar school. Writing couldn't have been further from my mind. I spent the summer holiday of 1961 laying crazy-paving paths all over the garden of my new house. Six weeks doing nothing but handling stones and mixing concrete! Such a waste of creative time seems appalling to me now. I suppose it was creative in a way; I was proud of it when I'd finished. But the writing had simply ceased to exist.

It came back to life one day in 1963. I went into the public library, and there was an exhibition of abstract paintings by a young engineer who had tired of building concrete structures and given up all for art. This touched me; besides, the pictures were rather good and very cheap. On an impulse I walked into the local newspaper office and asked the editor to give the young man a break with publicity. He said:

'OK, but nobody knows damn-all about art in this office. You're an art teacher, you write about it.'

He paid me two guineas for it, it was well received, and the young engineer sold half his pictures. Afterwards the editor, Geoff Moore, asked me to write a regular art review. I owe a lot to Geoff; he was a real old-time local editor who lived at his battered typewriter. He used to lean his elbows on it while he talked to you. He had round grooves in his elbow bones that fitted exactly into the frame of his typewriter. Talking on the phone he yelled so hard you learnt to hold the earpiece well away from your ear to avoid damaging your eardrums.

Geoff taught me brevity, to explain abstract art to the ordinary man-in-the-street in five hundred words and not one more (otherwise Geoff would cut my stuff in the most unfortunate places), and I honed my writing to a razor edge. I learnt never to use a long word when a short one would do. I had never been at all a difficult or obscure writer; now all my drive was to connect with the ordinary Joe as efficiently as possible. As the years went by, I spread my wings gently; articles on new public buildings; articles on good old buildings threatened by redevelopment (I managed to save one splendid Regency workhouse from demolition). Then work for magazines – architectural profiles of small towns mainly, with the odd human-interest in-depth profile. I spent a while as the northern art critic of the national *Guardian*, and wrote antiques articles for the national magazine *Homes and Gardens*. As a journalist I learnt to write crisply, interestingly and even amusingly. I think as a journalist I became a real pro.

As a novelist, when I began writing novels again, I remained a complete idiot, totally self-indulgent and writing in third-hand clichés about things I neither knew nor understood. I still have, in school exercise books, the tale of an Anglo-

Bob and Christopher at Westhall Church in Suffolk

Saxon princess travelling through seventh-century England to get married. After ninety-thousand words of rubbish she still hadn't reached her husband-to-be. I was later to while away long railway journeys with my son by reading him extracts; it was so comically dreadful that tears of laughter used to stream down his face.

I might have gone on writing trash for ever, but for something that happened as his twelfth birthday approached in 1972. We had been very close until, one morning in the holidays, a strange group of three boys appeared at our back door. I opened it. The boy at the front was amiable enough, but he had that air of authority and dignity that one sometimes sees in African tribal chiefs. The two other boys stood back at a respectful distance, not from me, but from him. They were obviously followers; even more obviously an escort or bodyguard. The chieftain enquired politely whether my son was in. I called Chris and the moment he saw this boy, he went berserk. He just grabbed his anorak and left with him, deaf to enquiries as to where he was going, or reminders that lunch was at one and that the family were going to town that afternoon. My wife and I were left with the uncomfortable feeling that we had ceased to exist. Christopher was about to be initiated into a gang.

Now do not get me wrong; this was not some dangerous and hooligan gang. I suppose 'tribe' would be a better word. Someone has said that childhood is the last primitive tribe that has not yet been conquered by civilization, and that fits the bill uncannily. In England such tribes find a vacant lot on the fringe of civilization: it must have no current occupant. An old overgrown garden or derelict allotment is best, with as much tree cover as possible. Here, they build a camp, or rather a house, of hardboard or corrugated iron, filched from rubbish tips or abandoned buildings; they are not so much thieves as snappers-up of unconsidered trifles such as bricks and sand from building sites.

Here, in the summer, the tribe lives, usually eight to ten strong. It marks out the boundaries of its territories and is acutely aware of, and usually at war with, the neighbouring tribes. Weapons are bizarre but not particularly lethal; sticks with nails in, bags of very wet mud or flour, water bombs. The purpose is to pillage and destroy the enemy camp, and drag away the booty. Frankly, I don't know what they'd find to do if it wasn't for this warfare, since much of their time is spent rebuilding ravaged camps. I would never have got to know all this, except my son's camp had trouble with a persistently leaking roof. The gang leader had read my architectural articles in the local paper and, after a great discussion, my son was sent to invite me to report to the gang headquarters.

I'll never forget approaching the territory at the prescribed hour. I was spotted far-off by a scout up a tree, who went racing off into the dense undergrowth. The chief appeared with two spear carriers, and I was escorted up to the well-hidden camp, feeling like a mixture between a hostage and a visiting ambassador.

Fortunately, I managed to spot the cause of the leak swiftly: they had overlapped their sheets of corrugated iron wrongly. (Had I failed I am certain my son would never have spoken to me again!) Afterwards I was invited to partake of a cup of rather weak tea boiled over an open fire. The interior of the camp was scrupulously tidy, and hilariously bourgeois, with pink armchairs thieved from a tip, a battered washing-up rack and even a battered black-and-white television set in pride of place. There was actually a roster of housework, willingly done, though the idea of any of them lifting a hand to help at home would have been risible.

The mixture of bourgeois surroundings mixed with utterly alien tribal coldness (even on the part of my son), can only be likened to that well-known photograph of the tamed Apache chief Geronimo sitting in a Model-T Ford, in his full tribal regalia. It would have been fatally easy to laugh, but had I not kept a perfectly straight face, I would have been banished into outer darkness for ever.

As it was, I was awarded honorary tribal membership, and my son was allowed to tell me all the secrets of the gang, otherwise he would have been sworn to a secrecy nothing would have broken. One of the gang had been frequently beaten by his father in an attempt to find the camp's whereabouts, and had taken all his punishment tight-lipped as an Apache under torture. I learnt about their tribal laws: they spent nearly as much time law-making as camp building, and even imported a sixteen-year old, paying him to act as an impartial judge. Punishments were graded from mild to severe, the worst being permanent expulsion from the gang; rather a dreadful punishment as the pariah was left exposed to the brutalities of all the surrounding gangs.

It was after all this that I began my own journey in memory back to the time when I was twelve, in the Second World War. I wanted to share childhoods with Christopher. Memories began to surface. A friend said, 'Why does the smell of burning kerosene make me feel safe?' and that carried me straight back to the air-raid shelters of my youth. Another time, after a particularly violent television war film, I went to sleep and dreamt, and wakening said to my wife, 'My war wasn't fought with tanks and planes and guns. My war was fought by old men and women and kids.' But I couldn't remember the content of the dream.

And then, suddenly, the whole time that I was twelve came back to me in one great surge of memory. The smells, the fears, what we ate: total recall. Only it wasn't a literary activity, it was a social activity. I wrote it in longhand, in school exercise books, and only intended to read it to my son. It was my gift to him, at the age he had reached; the age when boys in primitive tribes are initiated; the time when Jewish boys have their bar mitzvah. I read him the chapters as soon as I had written them, at Sunday teatime. He was the most savage of critics: if a part bored him he'd pick up a magazine and start reading that instead. The parts that left him cold, I crossed out, which is perhaps what gives the book its pace. But I had no thought of trying for publication. After we had finished reading the book out loud, I threw it into a drawer where it gathered dust until I lent it to a friend. It is, I suppose, ironical that a book written solely for one boy has sold over a million copies. However, in 1975 *The Machine-Gunners* was published, and through its publication I met my greatest editor, Marni Hodgkin.

I went to London to meet her. There was a little public park near her office at Macmillan. I sat on a seat and stared at the hopeful sparrows and smoked a cigarette to stop myself sweating and trembling. I smoked that cigarette so hard I felt like a blast furnace; it had a glowing coal on the end over an inch long. I felt I was taking my soul to the dentist, and it was going to hurt. Every other book we ever did, I felt the same; fond though I got of her, the feeling never got any better.

Like a condemned man I got up and walked into Macmillan's. Where I was subjected to the universal Ten Minute Wait. As I've become more successful my treatment by editors has changed in many ways. For instance, the new writer is fed sandwiches and coffee in the office; the Carnegie Medallist gets superb meals in restaurants where the menu is written in totally illegible Italian, where waiters appear to be trying to set fire to themselves at nearly every table, and where the bill, briefly glimpsed upside down, seems enough to feed an Ethiopian family for a year. But the Ten Minute Wait never changes. I often wonder what they do during it. Finish editing a piece of deathless prose or wash out the dirty coffee cups? Comb their hair and put on lipstick, or just sit gazing at their watches until the poor sucker downstairs is sufficiently softened up for their first approach with the editorial knife? If I met Solzhenitsyn, the first thing I'd ask is whether he got the same Ten Minute treatment. Certainly, arriving early, late or punctually makes no difference.

Finally, I was ushered into an office as small and packed with items as a 747 cockpit. Marni and Di Denney, her assistant editor, faced each other across two typewriters on two desks pushed together. Otherwise it was a cockpit composed entirely of paper. The upper walls were covered with posters from their most successful books. Then came the books themselves, row upon row, mostly open to display their jackets. Every horizontal surface was covered with proofs in various precarious stages of development and equilibrium, and every empty corner was filled with tottering towers of unsolicited manuscripts, as yet unread. These last, I discovered later, were the true cross they condemned themselves to bear. Every page of every unsolicited manuscript was read. Horrified at the prospect, I later suggested that they treat them as I treat a new book in the public library: read the first two pages, the last two, and a few half-pages between. I got a very dusty answer. In those brown stacks of unsoliciteds might be a grain of gold, a future Shakespeare. Even a half-page that promised gold must not be missed. I once heard Jill Paton Walsh, herself no mean book critic with the posh papers, ask Marni whether she might relieve her of some of the burden. Marni, suddenly for once tight-lipped, said:

'We are our own readers!'

But on that first day Di, with practised dexterity, was carving a small hole in the paper maze, and borrowing a canvas chair from next door on which I might sit down. But if the physical space was cramped, if one scarcely dared breathe for fear of sending Diana Wynne-Jones' next masterpiece tumbling across the floor in galley-proof ruin, the atmosphere was immense, august and grand. If one's body squirmed surreptitiously, one's mind began to fly free in endless circles in a kind of empyrean. One seemed to breathe the very air of Mount Parnassus, if not Mount Olympus. This was, I think, Marni's great gift as an editor. Not the fine chopping and knitting that is the normal work of an editor, paragraph by paragraph, line by line. She was good at that, but not quite as good as Di. No, it was that she provoked me into wild flights of fancy that could last an hour at a time, and from which, afterwards, when the wildness had cooled, came the books. I can only compare her to the kind of indulgent yet responsible aunt who will let a small boy show off on his bicycle by riding with no hands, and yet will quickly warn him if real danger threatens. With her I felt completely safe and totally let myself go. If *The Machine-Gunners* was written for my son alone, before I ever thought of being published, then *The Wind Eye* was written for Marni. Without her I would never have dared start a book that ends with a confrontation between a modern atheist Cambridge don and a time-travelling seventh-century saint. Totally mad, but for Marni's sake it worked. She was the last person who ever made me feel a wild impetuous young man and, at forty-four, that was like strong drink. I had this need to amaze her, even stupefy her with my flights of fancy; I used to ring her up when a new, raw idea hit me and gabble near-garbage on the phone for hours; and she, only moderately amazed, and certainly never stupefied, would begin gently patting the ideas into publishable shape. After she left Macmillan I wrote to her:

'Without you, I have no sense of assaulting Mount

Olympus any more; now we are just trying to make good books for children'.

But she had a magic, an audacity of her own. She cut away the whole first chapter of one book merely saying:

'It holds up the action simply to give the facts, and you give all the facts we need anyway in the next chapter.'

I gasped, as if she had suddenly beheaded my newborn child; but she was absolutely right; the headless corpse has been running happily ever since.

She had the capacity for instant and decisive manoeuvre, to turn on a pin, worthy of one of Napoleon's more successful marshals. When Di was thrown from a horse and broke her pelvis, Marni made a phone call to make sure of her welfare, then turned to the young woman writer she happened to be interviewing at that particular moment and said, 'Would you like a three-month job as my assistant?'

The arrangement, I gather, was a brilliant and instant success. Or so I was later told by the young woman writer, who enjoyed the experience hugely. All the stories one heard of Marni's triumphs were told by other people.

She always began our later meetings by asking in depth about my own life and times; so earnestly, as if I was a member of her family, that I sometimes wondered if we were ever going to start discussing the book at all. Then I would be told, with enormous concern and sympathy, how the other members of her 'writing' family were getting on; problems they were having with their books. So one never realized how little she ever talked about herself. I only knew she had a husband called Alan, because she sometimes told very funny 'Alan' jokes. The one I remember best was when, during the Queen's Silver Jubilee of 1977, Marni observed a strange large delta-winged shape flying over London. She went home and said to Alan:

'I saw a British bomber flying over London today – I'd never seen one before, so I think it must be new.'

'You never saw it before because it's so old,' said Alan. 'They daren't fly them very often, because they're worn out.'

A very English joke. But I was only told Alan was a Cambridge don after I had made a Cambridge don the hero of *The Wind Eye*, merely on the strength of having spent one weekend in Magdalen College, Oxford, and reading a life of Bertrand Russell.

'Why didn't you tell me,' I yelped, 'before I made a total fool of myself?'

'Because you'd never have dared write the book.'

'Was my don absolutely hopeless?'

'Oh, no, I've met plenty of dons just like him.'

Perhaps I began to realize then that that tiny paper-laden office, with its strangely heady atmosphere, was a tiny detached fragment of the greatness of Cambridge. Ideas and friendship were all; money, marketing, sales were never mentioned. Of course, elsewhere in the building there were good, kind, honest, trustworthy people who saw to those sorts of things properly; but we had a mutual wish never to discuss them; it got in the way of the real task. Once, purely because somebody else had asked me, I asked them how many copies of *The Machine-Gunners* I had sold. Marni and Di looked at each other, rather perplexed, as if I'd suddenly asked for the price of cod at Billingsgate Market. Di got a child's exercise book out of her drawer, ran her finger down a list of scrawled figures, and told me. Then we all breathed a sigh of relief and got back to business.

This may sound Dickensian today, but it was wise. In Marni's day, I was always flying off to see them in London on the slightest possible excuse; often with no excuse at all. And I was always welcome, like family. And inevitably, once I was in that office, I began to talk and the idea for the next book began to take shape in the air, and the most astonished person was me.

Now, I go to London as little as possible. My publishers since Marni and Di have been kind; they have dined me well and laughed at my jokes. But there is too much talk of sales and markets, of angles and target figures, of who is doing well, and who is not selling. I find it infinitely disturbing to my writing, so I stay away. Two of my latest books have been edited and published without my seeing the editors at all.

I suppose few people outside publishing realize how important editors are, and how closely they work with writers to make a book. The haggling, the bargaining that goes on between a book being accepted and being published would put the trade unions in the shade. Marni wanted changes, big and small. I could never tell before she asked for them how I would react. With some things I'd just laugh and say,

'You're quite right, how could I have been so silly, take it out.' Other times I'd roar, 'I'd die rather than take that out – that's what the whole book's about. I'd rather it wasn't published . . .'

Only to find she was smiling and holding up one hand in that famous soothing way. The haggling session about *The Wind Eye* went on for five hours and we came back to consciousness in a dark, empty and windy London, and we all began to wonder how we were possibly going to get home that night; we were too exhausted to stand until Di said,

'Shall I make a cup of tea?'

Usually, Marni got about half of the alterations she wanted. She told me once that Richard Adams wouldn't let anybody edit out a single word of *Watership Down*. When I read that book, although I admired it a great deal, I thought I saw quite a lot of passages where an editorial knife would have done some good.

She didn't have things all her own way, though. I once seduced her into writing two pages of dialogue for me. It was the dialogue of the young Jewess pawnbroker in *Fathom Five*. Once, as a child, I had ventured into a Jewish pawnbroker's, in search of a cheap pair of binoculars. I remembered the shop, the handsome Jewess, to perfection. But all I had said to her on that famous occasion was,

'Have you any binoculars for sale?' and she had said simply, 'No.'

Which didn't give me much grasp of Jewish diction, and I'd never consciously met a Jew since. So the words I put into my Jewess's mouth were about as real as a three-pound note, and this drove Marni, who as a New Yorker knew plenty of Jews, absolutely up the wall. And I refused to take the Jewess out (she only had a minor role) and Marni refused to accept my efforts. After about an hour of this irresistible force meeting an immovable object, Marni said wearily, 'OK' and the Jewish dialogue flowed from her like Moses smiting the rock in the wilderness.

I think she forgave me. Afterwards Di told me Marni had written four excellent crime thrillers in her maiden name, before taking up editing. Marni wouldn't have told me in a month of Sundays.

What I remember her for most though, is a terrible rigorous

honesty. Like when I got two simultaneous offers for the paperback rights to *The Machine-Gunners*. One was from the world-famous Penguin Books and the other was from her own Macmillan paperback house. She wrote, scrupulously laying out the pros and cons of both offers, and ended up,

'With Macmillan, you will get more money, in obscurity. With Penguin, you will get the kudos and fame. Now I leave you to make your own mind up . . .' On such foundations, whole worlds can stand.

Mind you, there were times when I smarted from such rigour, especially over the book *Fathom Five*, which Marni rejected as unpublishable about a week after I'd won the Carnegie Medal for *The Machine-Gunners*. She did say wryly that turning down a Carnegie Medallist was a new experience for her. Once again, it was a case of the irresistible force and the immovable object. I was determined to get *Fathom Five* published if it killed me. Five times, between writing other books, I rewrote it. Of the fourth rewrite she said,

'Good enough for Macmillan, but not good enough for Westall.'

So I said, 'OK. Tell me what's wrong with it.'

And with a weary heartfelt sigh she did. When it was finally published, all trace of our mutual agony vanished from it; it just fell into line with the others.

The end of our working relationship was swift. I opened *The Times* newspaper one morning to read that Sir Alan Hodgkin, the Nobel Prize-winning scientist, had been made Master of Trinity College, Cambridge. At last, the 'Alan' of the jokes stood revealed, after all those years. The blow soon followed. Marni was leaving publishing for eighteen months 'to help Alan settle in'. I could guess the rest. Trinity is probably the most prestigious of all the Cambridge colleges. The previous Master, Rab Butler, had nearly been British prime minister, but lost to Edward Heath. Prince Charles had gone to Trinity: it was as much a political and social as an academic appointment. I doubted Marni (I still couldn't get the words 'Lady Hodgkin' round my tongue) would ever come back. And I was right; she found Cambridge even more fascinating than publishing.

But that isn't quite the end. At Macmillan, and then at Chatto, Di and I struggled to keep the old firm afloat, frequently laughing at the way we still did things 'Marni's way'. And then over *Futuretrack Five* we totally failed to see eye to eye. It was a violent, angry book; every ounce of anger I felt as a careers teacher about what the Tory government was doing to my children went into it; it was a picture of the twenty-first century, of a Tory government gone berserk, using drugs and gang wars, motorbikes and sex, to kill off the teenagers it couldn't find jobs for. Di said it was no good, unpublishable. I just knew it was what I had to say. That's always been my trouble; when I write a book as a light-hearted lark it invariably does well; when I write from deep and bitter feelings I go left-wing and angry, and that book's in trouble.

Anyway, after a long and hopeless session, Di and I looked at each other, and we both said 'Marni' in unison. Marni would be the judge between us. Out of friendship, she did it; as rigorously honest as ever. She hated the book; she thought I ought to throw it on the scrapheap. But here were three names of publishers who would certainly publish it.

The first publisher took it: it got a Carnegie nomination. It will have become obvious by now that Marni is

American. To me, she represents the Other America. All intelligent Brits have this dream of the 'Other America'. The America of Henry James and T.S. Eliot, the Roosevelts, and the Kennedys, the *New Yorker* magazine, Dorothy Parker, James Thurber, Ogden Nash – a very elegant, rather English America. We delight in the quiet stooping Midwest lecturer who just happens to know and love our English churches better than we do ourselves. We dream of meeting such people, and as we are hit by waves of TV programmes like *Dallas* and *Kojak* we feel lonelier and lonelier, and the old English-speaking Union seems to get further and further away. Marni always seemed to me to belong with that America; she was and is a marvellous ambassador.

I seem to see resemblances between Marni and Henry Moore. When Marni stumbled on the cobbles of Dr Johnson's house because she could never remember to have the heels of her shoes repaired, I remembered Henry Moore's ex-Navy sweater. Marni's eyes were on children's literature as Moore's were on sculpture; they both rejoiced in the talent they found in others, and rather hid their own under a bushel, until it came to the crunch, when they both had that rock-like, bruising integrity. At least, I can think of worse recipes for greatness. When I look around the world and see the would-be great kneeing, gouging, telling public lies for their own advantage, clawing each other's eyes out in public and private, telling sly stories behind each other's backs, I find my two very restful to ponder on.

There is really very little more to tell. Since then, I have simply been doing more of the same. It is the story of everyday, and writers' everydays are not thrilling at all, much less than those of pilots or deep-sea divers.

Postscript

Robert Westall wrote forty-eight books. Twelve of these have been published posthumously. His work won him the following prizes and shortlists:

1975 *The Machine-Gunners*:
  Carnegie Medal
  Runner-up for *Guardian* Award
  (American) *Boston Globe Horn Book* Honor Book (1977)

1979 *The Devil on the Road*:
  Runner-up Carnegie Medal

1982 *The Scarecrows*:
  Carnegie Medal (The first writer to win it a second time.)
  (American) *Boston Globe Horn Book* Honor Book (1982)

1983 *Futuretrack Five*:
  Observer/Malcolm Bradbury Top Ten

1987 *Urn Burial*:
  Runner-up Children's Book Prize

1989 *Blitzcat*:
  Smarties Senior Prize
  Runner-up Children's Book Prize
The Machine-Gunners:
  Preis der Leseratten (German)

1990 *The Kingdom by the Sea*:
  The *Guardian* Award
  Carnegie Highly Commended
The Promise:
  Sheffield Children's Book Prize
Futuretrack Five:
  Preis der Leseratten (German)

1991 *Yaxley's Cat*:
  Carnegie Medal shortlist
  Smarties Prize shortlist
The Promise:
  Preis der Leseratten (German)

1992 *Gulf*:
  Carnegie Medal Highly Commended
  Whitbread Prize shortlist
  Joint Winner Lancashire Children's Book Prize
  Children's Book Award Longer Novel Category Winner

The Stones of Muncaster Cathedral:
  The Dracula Society 'Children of the Night' Award

Robert Westall died on 15 April 1993, aged sixty-three in hospital in Warrington, Cheshire. His ashes are buried in Northwich, Cheshire. He is commemorated in Seven Stories, the Centre for Children's Books in Newcastle-upon-Tyne, where there is a Robert Westall Gallery.

Bibliography

Chapter Seven
'A Whole World' by Robert Westall
First published in *Best of Friends*, edited by Valerie
Bierman. Methuen Children's Books 1995

Chapter Ten
'Fifty-fafty' by Robert Westall
First published in *Hidden Turnings*, edited by Diana
Wynne-Jones. Methuen Children's Books 1989

'Something About the Author' (Volume 2), an
Autobiographical Series, published by the Gale Research
Company, Detroit, Michigan, USA 1986

Children of the Blitz by Robert Westall
First published by Viking 1985

About Lindy McKinnel

I first met Robert Westall at a children's party in 1966 in Northwich, Cheshire to which his only son, Christopher and my twin daughters had been invited. Our children went to the same school and eventually our two families became friends. I discovered that Bob (as he was always called) wrote in his spare time and I started to read his architectural articles which appeared in the magazine 'Cheshire Life', complete with his drawings of buildings. This sparked an interest in architecture which has never left me but it also meant that, after a year or so, Bob began to give me all kinds of pieces that he had written including his first attempts at novels. His writing varied a great deal but I did encourage him and when, in 1973, he showed me the manuscript of 'The Machine Gunners' which he had written entirely for Christopher in school exercise books, I suggested that he try for publication. He sent it off to Collins who promptly turned it down. I felt incensed because it was such a good story but Macmillan took it, it won Bob his first Carnegie Medal in 1975 and has since become a children's classic.

In 1969 I had moved away to Lymm after the death of my husband at the early age of forty-seven and Bob and his wife were very supportive of my efforts to raise my four children alone. However, tragedy struck them too in 1978 when Christopher was killed riding his motorbike at the age of eighteen. This was completely devastating. There is no doubt that Christopher was the inspiration behind Bob's early writing but, to make matters worse, it had appalling consequences for Jean, Bob's wife. His death exacerbated the mental health problems she already suffered, serious illness followed with only a partial recovery and restricted mobility. Over the next nine difficult years the marriage broke down, followed by separation, divorce and, sadly, Jean's eventual suicide.

These years had a deep effect on Bob and he became a 'workaholic', holding down two jobs at the school where he taught (Head of Art and Head of Careers) as well as filling up his spare time with writing. He wrote his short stories as and when they occurred to him and his longer novels in the school holidays. I was given all his work to read and he asked for my opinion which he must have valued as I tried to be honest both in encouragement and in criticism. I had always enjoyed reading his work but I felt that some of his writing was brilliant. In 1985 after the death of both his parents within six months of each other he took the opportunity for early retirement and opened a little antique shop. Antiques had always interested him and he wrote articles about them which appeared in the local newspaper. I too was interested in antiques but our tastes did not always coincide. He liked large objects, big furniture, chairs and he was mad about clocks. My taste was for smaller objects, tables, Victorian paperweights and small Staffordshire figures, but I also liked clocks.

In 1987 Bob separated from his wife and came to live in Lymm with me. By this time he had had about twelve books published and had won the Carnegie again with *The*

Scarecrows. He had become an established children's writer. Life in Lymm seemed to suit him: while I was out at work registering births, marriages and deaths, Bob wrote. Books poured out of him. Literary awards flowed in. We had fun incorporating some of the names I had registered into his short stories ('Warren, Sharron and Darren') and he wrote an entertaining spooky story entitled *Beelzebub* about the registration of a very odd baby. He had brought a beloved cat with him called Jeoffrey who, luckily, settled down happily with my two cats. Cat stories were written. The quality of his work inevitably varied but he seemed to have so much that he wanted to say and, perceptively in retrospect, not a great deal of time in which to say it.

He was having four books published a year and a multiplicity of editors, visitors and an agent all started to come to see him. In addition the continuing acquisition of clocks and chairs from our forays to antique fairs meant that my small house began to seem overcrowded. This problem was alleviated by the purchase of a nearby cottage as I had put an embargo on the erection of a shed for writing in my small garden. The cottage proved to be a great success and it too soon became filled with more furniture and books and, by the end, the clock total had risen to somewhere in the seventies! The cottage also proved an ideal workplace as a venue in which to entertain the callers. The upstairs bedroom became a useful overflow for visiting members of my own family who, by now, had left home and started work and were acquiring girlfriends, boyfriends, husbands and, in 1992 my first grandchild. The whole set-up became, truly, a 'cottage industry' and Bob started to complain that there was no time for his creative writing. The pile of fan letters had become mountainous, the requests for speaking and visiting poured in, the proofs needed to be corrected and the commissions started coming in: in short he needed some help. As luck would have it I reached the age of sixty in 1992 and was therefore in a position to retire from my job in registration. I took up a new post as writer's general dogsbody. Little did I suspect how useful this career move was going to be. Besides now reading all the writing, I was entrusted with typing up radio plays, dealing with general correspondence and other mundane tasks. I succeeded in learning the names of all the different editors and which publishers they belonged to and life was never dull. Sometimes, when we went to the cinema, a very popular occupation, I just fell asleep from fatigue.

However, Bob had been a heavy smoker all his life and his chest was undoubtedly 'wheezy'. Doctors didn't figure in his life style despite my best efforts. In 1993 he contracted a virus which so rapidly turned to pneumonia that he suffered a respiratory arrest. With a doctor on the way I suddenly found myself attempting to give him mouth-to-mouth resuscitation by instruction on the telephone from the ambulance service. He never regained consciousness and died in the local hospital on 15th April 1993. I felt completely shattered. Several books were in various stages of publication, fan mail poured daily through the letterbox together with all the many requests that his work engendered and there was no-one to deal with it except me. Somehow I coped. My workload was huge. The funeral took place and, later, a Memorial service which took a lot of planning. Correspondence needed answering, publishing decisions made, proofs required correcting and two houses had to be run. Bob's agent, Laura Cecil, his literary executor was

enormously supportive though I scarcely knew her to start
with, and one of his editors, the late Miriam Hodgson,
helped me through the early grieving process.

As his only beneficiary there was, however, something that
I could do. I decided to set up The Robert Westall Charitable
Trust with money from his estate. I wanted to ensure that
he and his work would not be forgotten and that something
of lasting value be created that Bob himself would have
appreciated. I did not know what this would be. Strangely,
I did not have to wait long. I soon learned through the late
Miriam Hodgson of Elizabeth Hammill's dream to found
a Centre for Children's Books where the manuscripts of
British children's writers and illustrators might be housed
and their work celebrated, there not being anywhere else
in Britain for this purpose. It seemed to me to be a very
reprehensible state of affairs that this country did not value
these documents, many of which were being sold abroad.
I told Elizabeth that I would back her with the £100,000
in the Trust and this action kick-started the long fund-
raising process which eventually culminated, in 2005, in the
opening of Seven Stories, the Centre for Children's Books
in the Ouseburn Valley in Newcastle-upon-Tyne, not more
than ten miles from where Bob had been born in 1929. One
of the galleries bears his name, The Robert Westall Gallery.
His archive, which is currently on permanent loan to Seven
Stories, will be given to the Centre on my death.

Seven Stories, the Centre for Children's Books

Seven Stories, based in the Ouseburn Valley, Newcastle-upon-Tyne provides the only exhibition space in the UK wholly dedicated to the work of British children's writers and illustrators. Recognised as a new national home for children's literature, it brings together original manuscripts and artwork from some of the nation's best loved children's books.

The Centre invites visitors of all ages to engage in a unique, interactive exploration of creativity, literature and art. In this literary playgound, they can become writers, artists, explorers, designers, storytellers, readers or collectors, in the company of storytellers, authors, illustrators and other facilitators.

As part of Seven Stories rolling programme of exhibitions **Westall's Kingdom: a writer's life** celebrates Robert Westall's work running through October 2006 to summer 2007. Visitors are invited to explore the wonderful books Robert Westall created, and delve into nostalgic Tyneside reflecting what it was like growing up during the war. Visitors will at once connect with the books and be led through an eye-catching, thought-provoking exhibition.

For more information and details of events log onto the website www.sevenstories.org.uk or call 0845 271 0777.